Computational Intelligence for Alzheimer's Detection

By
Trevor Philips

TABLE OF CONTENTS

CHAPTER NO.	TITLE	PAGE NO.
CHAPTER 1	**INTRODUCTION**	**1**
	1.1 Background	1
	1.2 Motivation	3
	1.3 Problem statement	4
	1.4 Objectives of the study	5
	1.5 Research Gaps	6
	1.6 Scope and significance	7
	1.7 Overview of the thesis	10
	1.8 Ethical, Societal, and Practical considerations in AI-based Alzheimer's Diagnosis	10
	1.9 Summary	12
CHAPTER 2	**LITERATURE REVIEW**	**14**
	2.1 Review of machine learning for Alzheimer's disease	14
	2.2 Review of deep learning and multimodal frameworks	29
	2.3 Critical analysis of research gaps	49
	2.4 Future research directions in AI-based Alzheimer's Detection	53
	2.5 Explainable Artificial Intelligence (XAI) and Interpretability in Alzheimer's Disease Research	54
	2.6 Summary	55

CHAPTER 3		**MATERIALS AND METHODS**	**57**
	3.1	Dataset description	57
	3.2	Data Preprocessing	59
		3.2.1 MRI Data Preprocessing	59
		3.2.2 Clinical data preprocessing	61
	3.3	Applied Machine learning models	63
	3.4	Applied Deep learning models	66
		3.4.1 CNN Baseline	66
		3.4.2 Transfer learning models	68
	3.5	MRI dataset classes	73
	3.6	Proposed Architecture	74
		3.6.1 Algorithm	77
		3.6.2 Mathematical model	78
		3.6.3 Computational Complexity Analysis	80
	3.7	Performance metrics	81
	3.8	Experimental Setup	83
	3.9	Summary	85
CHAPTER 4		**RESULTS AND DISCUSSION**	**86**
	4.1	Alzheimer's prediction using ML models	86
	4.2	Results on MRI using DL models	101
	4.3	Results analysis for proposed Architecture: AlzFusionNet	105
	4.4	Comparative Discussion with State-of-the-Art Models	108
		4.4.1 Comparison with recent 2024-2025 studies	109
	4.5	Explainability and Clinical Relevance Analysis	110
	4.6	Summary of Findings	111

CHAPTER 1: INTRODUCTION

1.1 BACKGROUND

Alzheimer's disease (AD) is one of the most devastating neurodegenerative disorders of our time. It is the leading cause of dementia and is characterized by progressive loss of memory, reasoning, and cognitive abilities that gradually erode a person's independence. The disease predominantly affects older adults, with the likelihood of occurrence doubling approximately every five years after the age of 65 [4]. According to the World Health Organization (WHO), more than 57 million people are currently living with Alzheimer's or other dementias, and this figure is projected to rise to 153 million by 2050 [3].

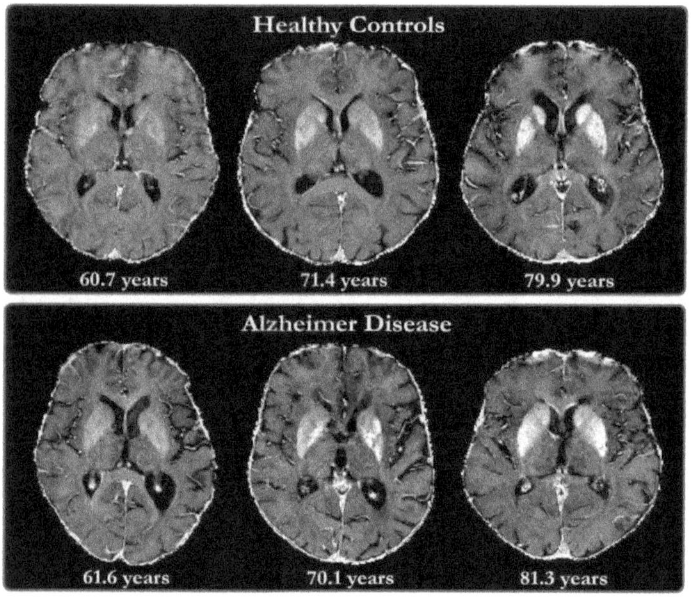

Figure 1.1: Brain Iron accumulation in Alzheimer's disease

Such alarming growth poses a severe strain on global healthcare systems, caregivers, and socio-economic structures. The burden of Alzheimer's extends beyond the patient it affects families, healthcare professionals, and society through immense emotional, social, and economic costs.

At the biological level, Alzheimer's disease is associated with two pathological hallmarks: amyloid-beta (Aβ) plaques and neurofibrillary tangles composed of hyperphosphorylated tau proteins [17, 25]. These abnormal accumulations lead to synaptic dysfunction, neuronal death, and widespread brain atrophy, particularly in the hippocampus and cortex regions.

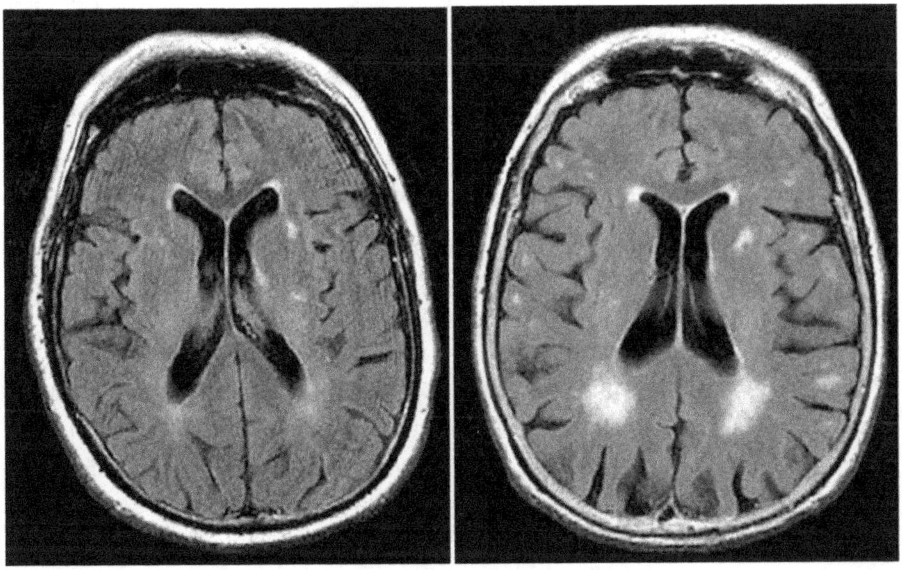

Figure 1.2: Brain MRI risk reveals for Alzheimer's diseases

Despite decades of research, there is still no definitive cure for Alzheimer's disease, and available treatments only provide symptomatic relief rather than halting or reversing neurodegeneration. Therefore, early detection and diagnosis are vital to slow the progression, enable timely interventions, and improve patients' quality of life.

Traditional methods of diagnosing Alzheimer's involve a combination of clinical evaluations, neuropsychological testing, and neuroimaging. Tools such as the Mini-Mental State Examination (MMSE), Clinical Dementia Rating (CDR), and cognitive behavior assessments are widely used to assess mental functioning. Neuroimaging techniques, including Magnetic Resonance Imaging (MRI), Computed Tomography (CT), and Positron Emission Tomography (PET), provide visual evidence of structural and functional abnormalities in the brain. However, these conventional methods have several limitations. Clinical assessments are often subjective, vary between evaluators, and may fail to detect subtle changes in the early stages of the disease. Imaging studies, though objective, are resource-intensive, costly, and not always accessible in developing regions. Moreover, interpreting complex neuroimaging data requires significant expertise, which can limit scalability in clinical settings.

Recent advances in artificial intelligence (AI), particularly in machine learning (ML) and deep learning (DL), have opened new avenues for addressing these diagnostic challenges. AI systems have the capability to analyze vast amounts of heterogeneous data such as medical images, demographic details, genetic markers, and cognitive scores to uncover hidden relationships that may be imperceptible to human experts. Deep neural networks, especially convolutional neural networks (CNNs), have shown remarkable success in medical image analysis tasks like tumor detection, lesion segmentation, and disease classification. In the context of Alzheimer's disease, AI models have been employed to classify MRI scans, predict disease stages, and even forecast cognitive decline over time.

While these advances are promising, the majority of current models are unimodal, focusing solely on imaging or clinical data. This approach often overlooks the complementary information present in multiple data sources. For example, MRI scans capture anatomical and structural details of the brain, while clinical assessments provide behavioral and functional insights. Combining both can potentially offer a more comprehensive picture of disease progression. However, challenges such as data imbalance, interpretability, and multimodal fusion remain open research questions. This backdrop provides a compelling rationale for developing a robust, explainable, and scalable multimodal AI framework that can integrate diverse data streams for more accurate and early detection of Alzheimer's disease.

1.2 MOTIVATION

Alzheimer's disease (AD) is one of the most challenging and heartbreaking neurodegenerative disorders of our time. It gradually erodes memory, thinking ability, and daily functioning, eventually leading to complete dependence on caregivers. According to the World Health Organization, over 57 million people worldwide are currently living with dementia, and this number is expected to reach nearly 153 million by 2050. Among all forms of dementia, Alzheimer's disease accounts for around 60–70% of cases, making it a major global health concern with deep social and economic implications.

Despite ongoing research, there is still no permanent cure for Alzheimer's disease. Current pharmacological and non-pharmacological treatments provide only temporary relief and are primarily aimed at managing symptoms such as memory loss, confusion, and behavioral changes. Drugs like donepezil, rivastigmine, and memantine may help improve cognitive function for a short duration, but they cannot stop or reverse the underlying neurodegenerative process. Similarly, lifestyle-based interventions including cognitive training, diet modification, and physical activity have shown some benefit in delaying progression, yet their effectiveness remains limited to the early stages of the disease. Because of these therapeutic constraints, the focus of global Alzheimer's research has shifted toward early diagnosis and predictive modeling.

Early and accurate detection of Alzheimer's disease has the potential to transform patient care and clinical outcomes. Identifying the disease before significant neuronal loss occurs allows for the timely initiation of therapeutic and lifestyle interventions, which may slow cognitive decline and extend the period of independence for patients. Moreover, early detection provides families and caregivers with more time to plan for future care needs, participate in clinical trials, and adopt preventive strategies that improve long-term well-being. From a healthcare perspective, accurate early diagnosis also enables clinicians to stratify patients based on disease stage, personalize treatment plans, and optimize resource allocation. Therefore, advancing methods for early detection especially through Artificial Intelligence (AI)-driven approaches that analyze subtle imaging and clinical patterns represents one of the most promising directions in modern Alzheimer's research.

However, traditional diagnostic methods such as neuropsychological tests, MRI and PET scans, and clinical evaluations are often expensive, time-consuming, and sometimes subjective. Moreover, they tend to struggle with early-stage detection, where structural or cognitive changes are subtle and hard to identify.

Recent advances in Artificial Intelligence (AI), particularly Machine Learning (ML) and Deep Learning (DL), have shown great promise in medical diagnostics. AI-based systems can analyse complex imaging and clinical data to uncover patterns that are difficult for the human eye to detect. MRI imaging, in particular, has proven valuable for studying structural brain changes associated with Alzheimer's, while machine learning models can process clinical data such as cognitive scores, demographics, and behavioural measures.

However, most existing approaches use either imaging or clinical data in isolation, which limits the accuracy and generalization of predictions. This research is therefore motivated by the need to develop a robust multimodal diagnostic framework that can combine both clinical and MRI-based features to identify Alzheimer's disease at its earliest stages. Such an approach aims to enhance diagnostic reliability, provide better interpretability for clinicians, and ultimately contribute toward improved patient outcomes.

1.3 PROBLEM STATEMENT

Detecting Alzheimer's disease accurately remains a major challenge due to the complex nature of the disease and the diversity of available data. Traditional diagnostic systems are often limited by human subjectivity, while computational models must handle noisy, imbalanced, and heterogeneous datasets. Although a range of machine learning and deep learning models such as ExtraTree, Random Forest, Support Vector Machine (SVM), AdaBoost, CNNs, VGG16, ResNet, and EfficientNet have been applied to Alzheimer's classification tasks, most focus only on binary classification (demented vs. non-demented). These models often fail to distinguish finer stages of disease progression, such as very mild, mild, and moderate dementia, which are critical for clinical decision-making. Furthermore, existing models typically rely on either clinical or MRI data alone, which prevents them from capturing the full clinical picture of the disease. The lack of explainability and interpretability in many AI models also reduces their acceptability among medical professionals. Hence, this research addresses the problem of designing a multimodal AI framework capable of integrating both MRI-based imaging data and clinical features to perform fine-grained classification of Alzheimer's disease. The goal is to build a scalable, explainable, and efficient model that can improve diagnostic performance and assist healthcare providers in early detection and staging of Alzheimer's disease.

1.4 OBJECTIVES OF THE STUDY

The primary goal of this research is to develop an AI-driven multimodal framework (AlzFusionNet) for accurate and interpretable classification of Alzheimer's disease stages by combining MRI and clinical data.

The specific objectives are:

1. To collect and preprocess multimodal Alzheimer's datasets containing MRI scans and clinical parameters from established sources such as Open Access Series of Imaging Studies (OASIS), Alzheimer's Disease Neuroimaging Initiative (ADNI), and Kaggle.

2. To apply and evaluate a variety of machine learning models as ExtraTree, Random Forest, XGBoost, Gradient Boosting, Decision Tree, Linear Discriminant Analysis (LDA), Quadratic Discriminant Analysis (QDA), Logistic Regression, Naïve Bayes, SVM, Multi-Layer Perceptron (MLP), etc., for early detection using clinical features.

3. To analyze the performance of deep learning models such as CNN, VGG16, ResNet, AlexNet, and EfficientNet-B7 for MRI-based classification of Alzheimer's disease stages.

4. To design and implement the proposed AlzFusionNet model that integrates MRI-derived features from EfficientNet-B7 with clinical data through a fusion mechanism for multi-stage classification.

5. To compare and benchmark the proposed approach against traditional ML and DL models using Accuracy, Precision, Recall, F1-score, and Receiver Operating Characteristic – Area Under Curve (ROC-AUC) metrics.

6. To validate the model's generalization, scalability, and explainability, ensuring its potential for use in clinical and real-world diagnostic settings.

1.5 RESEARCH GAPS

Although several studies have explored AI-driven diagnosis of Alzheimer's disease, several gaps still remain:

- Many existing systems rely solely on single-modality data (either clinical or MRI), limiting their diagnostic potential.

- The majority of existing research focuses on binary classification, ignoring finer sub-stages that are clinically important.

- Models frequently suffer from data imbalance and overfitting, especially in small medical datasets.
- Explainability and interpretability are often lacking, making clinical adoption difficult.
- Few studies have explored hybrid or multimodal architectures that combine both clinical and imaging features in a unified model.
- Validation across large-scale and diverse datasets is still limited, restricting generalization to real-world conditions.

The proposed AlzFusionNet model seeks to bridge these gaps by combining imaging and clinical data through a deep learning-based fusion approach that enhances accuracy, generalization, and interpretability.

1.6 SCOPE AND SIGNIFICANCE

The scope of this research is centered on developing and evaluating an AI-driven multimodal framework, termed AlzFusionNet, that integrates MRI imaging features and clinical data for early-stage detection and fine-grained classification of Alzheimer's disease. The system seeks to narrow the diagnostic distance from imaging-only and clinical-only models by building a shared predictive framework that takes advantage of their assets. In this circumscribed domain, the research covers the following dimensions:

1. The publicly available and benchmark datasets OASIS, ADNI, and Kaggle dementia datasets are used for experimentation. These datasets contain MRI scans and the related clinical data, including MMSE, CDR scores and demographics. The multimodal integration allows the system to model complicated relationships between structural brain changes and cognitive symptoms.
2. EfficientNet-B7 was adopted as the basic DL framework for MRI feature emulation, thanks to its extensive capability and scalability in medical images tasks. It exhibits the layers for feature normalization, regularization, and dimension reduction. There is another branch of dense neural network that takes the clinical data into account, and they are fused in later stage to generate a meta feature representation: Mild Demented, Moderate Demented, Very Mild Demented, Non-Demented. The system's performance

is evaluated using standard metrics such as accuracy, precision, recall, F1-score, and ROC-AUC.

3. In addition to performance evaluation, the research emphasizes interpretability and clinical relevance by incorporating explainable AI (XAI) techniques such as Grad-CAM visualization and feature importance mapping. These methods help identify the most influential brain regions and clinical attributes contributing to model predictions, thereby enhancing transparency and trust in the AI system. This interpretability ensures that AlzFusionNet not only achieves high diagnostic accuracy but also provides meaningful insights that can assist neurologists and radiologists in understanding disease progression and making informed clinical decisions.

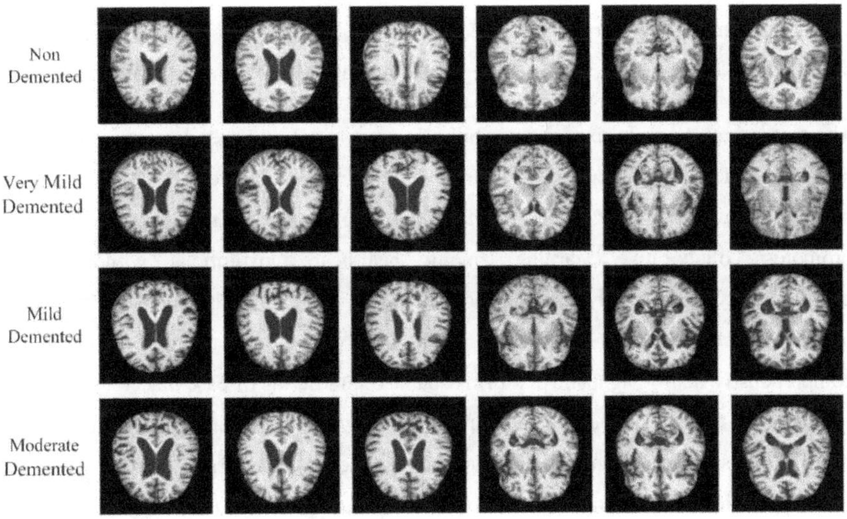

Figure 1.3: Different stages of Alzheimer's

4. The research is designed for experimental validation rather than full clinical deployment. The model is trained and tested using high-performance computational resources, but future work envisions optimizing it for real-world applications in healthcare settings. Ethical considerations, such as patient privacy and data anonymization, are maintained throughout.

The significance of this study lies in its contribution to both the academic and clinical domains. From an academic perspective, the proposed framework advances multimodal deep learning research by introducing an explainable architecture that fuses heterogeneous medical data effectively. From a clinical standpoint, it provides a foundation for the development of early diagnostic tools that could assist neurologists in identifying patients at risk before irreversible neuronal damage occurs. The fusion-based approach ensures higher diagnostic precision and interpretability, fostering trust among healthcare professionals.

In addition to its methodological and diagnostic objectives, the scope of this study extends toward translational applicability and scalability in real-world healthcare systems. The proposed framework, AlzFusionNet, can be adapted for hospital-based deployment as a clinical decision-support system (CDSS). This integration will enable neurologists to access rapid diagnostic suggestions derived from multimodal patient data, reducing turnaround time for early intervention. Furthermore, the model can be continuously retrained with institution-specific data, ensuring adaptability to regional populations and imaging protocols.

The research also emphasizes sustainability in computational healthcare, encouraging cloud-based or federated implementations that minimize data transfer while maintaining data sovereignty within hospitals. This not only strengthens patient data protection but also promotes collaborative learning among healthcare institutions without breaching confidentiality. Additionally, the multimodal learning pipeline can be expanded to include PET imaging, genetic markers, or longitudinal follow-up data, thereby evolving into a comprehensive neurodiagnostic platform capable of predicting disease trajectory and treatment response. By focusing on adaptability, interpretability, and ethical integration, the scope of this research transcends academic exploration paving the way for responsible AI deployment in clinical practice and forming a foundational step toward precision neurology.

Moreover, the study has broader implications for the healthcare ecosystem. The integration of AI into Alzheimer's diagnostics can reduce diagnostic delays, minimize costs associated with extensive manual evaluations, and enhance accessibility for patients in underserved regions. As the global burden of dementia continues to rise, such AI-assisted diagnostic systems could play a pivotal role in advancing precision medicine and improving public health outcomes.

1.7 OVERVIEW OF THE THESIS

This thesis is organized into five chapters:

- **Chapter 1: Introduction**

  Provides the overall background, motivation, research problem, objectives, and identified research gaps of the study.

- **Chapter 2: Literature Review**

  Presents a comprehensive review of previous studies on Alzheimer's detection using machine learning and deep learning methods, along with critical analysis of their limitations.

- **Chapter 3: Materials and Methods**

  Describes the datasets, preprocessing techniques, applied ML and DL models, and explains the architecture and methodology of the proposed AlzFusionNet framework.

- **Chapter 4: Results and Discussion**

  Includes experimental results, performance evaluation, comparison with existing models, and interpretation of outcomes through visual and statistical analysis.

- **Chapter 5: Conclusion and Future Work**

  Summarizes the research contributions, key findings, and offers directions for future work such as model enhancement, multimodal integration, and deployment in clinical practice.

1.8 ETHICAL, SOCIETAL, AND PRACTICAL CONSIDERATIONS IN AI-BASED ALZHEIMER'S DIAGNOSIS

The integration of Artificial Intelligence (AI) in medical diagnostics introduces not only technical advancements but also ethical and societal responsibilities. Alzheimer's disease research, which involves sensitive neuroimaging data and clinical information, requires stringent ethical frameworks to ensure patient privacy, data protection, and fairness. One of the foremost ethical concerns in AI-assisted diagnostics is data privacy. Medical datasets often contain identifiable health information, including MRI scans and demographic attributes, which must be anonymized and stored securely. Compliance with international standards such as the Health Insurance Portability and Accountability Act (HIPAA) and the General Data Protection Regulation (GDPR) is essential to safeguard patient confidentiality.

Another critical aspect involves bias and fairness in AI models. Training data often underrepresents specific groups based on ethnicity, gender, or socio-economic background, which can lead to biased predictions. These discrepancies may inadvertently contribute to inequality in access to health care or misdiagnosis rates for communities. Hence, creating balanced and diverse datasets as well as auditing AI models regularly to ensure fairness is essential in fair medical decision-making. Methods such as bias aware learning and federated training further mitigate systemic bias by promoting distributed model learning across facilities without exposing sensitive data.

It is equally important that AI models are interpretable and transparent. Networking experts attribute decision-making to some set of well-understood features, clinicians need to grasp the 'why' of an algorithm's prediction none more so than in high-stakes decisions like Alzheimer's staging. Explanation AI (XAI) frameworks like Grad-CAM, Shapley Additive exPlanations (SHAP), or Local Interpretable Model-agnostic Mapping (LIME) can shed light on the brain regions and clinical features that contribute to guide the model assessment. This transparency fosters clinician trust, leaving AI as a supportive tool rather than an opaque authority. Our AlzFusionNet framework will integrate visualization-based interpretability to visualize important MRI regions (e.g., hippocampus, cortex), aligned with predicted disease stages, making sure that cognitive reasoning and medical interpretation are in parallel.

From the perspective of society, an AI-driven Alzheimer's disease diagnosis can be a game changer in healthcare delivery. Automated screening aids can potentially decrease the reliance on expert neurologists and permit early detection even in resource-poor areas. Nevertheless, implementation must take into account infrastructure readiness, computing facilities, and physician preparation. The integration of such systems into the current hospital information systems requires a standardized data pipeline, interfacing with medical standards (e.g., Digital Imaging and Communications in Medicine (DICOM), Fast Healthcare Interoperability Resources (FHIR)) and seamless clinical-experience between AI developers and healthcare actors.

There is also ethic- psychological and communicative-effects. These and other factors highlight the need to be grounded in empathy and cautious when sharing AI-aided diagnosis findings with subjects, particularly those affected by a progressive neurodegenerative condition. The writer's role as a mediator in between modern technology and clients becomes essential in translating AI findings into sympathetic care.

Finally, engagements, policies resilience and accountability ought to be built into the deploy of AI. Ongoing surveillance of the model and retraining with new data followed by external validation is critical to avoid model decay. In addition, the creation of ethical committees or interdisciplinary review boards for AI healthcare systems can also serve to exert ongoing oversight of technological progress vis-à-vis human well-being.

In conclusion, ethical AI in Alzheimer's diagnostics should be guided by three principles: transparency, equity, and accountability to ensure that technological innovation advances human-centred healthcare.

1.9 SUMMARY

This chapter presented a comprehensive introduction to the research on Artificial Intelligence (AI)-driven early detection and classification of Alzheimer's disease (AD). The study's background and motivation were briefly discussed, along with the increasing global prevalence of AD, it's devastating effects on cognition and society, and the shortcomings of traditional diagnostic methods like clinical assessment and neuroimaging interpretation. According to the discussion, conventional methods can identify changes in the structure and function of the brain, but they frequently have trouble spotting the early, subtle patterns linked to the onset of disease.

The study's well-defined goals were to create and validate AlzFusionNet, a unified AI-based framework that aims to increase diagnostic accuracy across the various stages of Alzheimer's disease progression. It addressed important research gaps like reliance on single-modality datasets, poor generalization to real-world clinical scenarios, data imbalance, and limited model interpretability.

Furthermore, the research's importance and scope were explained to emphasize its dual impact of enhancing academic knowledge and providing real clinical advantages. The study advances explainable AI (XAI) and multimodal deep learning approaches from an educational perspective. Through the integration of clinical and MRI data, it aims to support neurologists and radiologists by offering more precise, dependable, and interpretable diagnostic predictions. Furthermore, the ethical and societal implications section highlights the need for responsible AI implementation by emphasizing the concepts of privacy, fairness, transparency, and equitable access to AI-driven diagnostic advancements in healthcare.

In summary, Chapter 1 established the foundation and rationale for the study defining its motivation, objectives, challenges, and intended contributions. It justified the development of AlzFusionNet as a comprehensive, interpretable, and scalable multimodal diagnostic framework. The next chapter, Chapter 2: Literature Review, builds upon this foundation by critically analyzing existing research in machine learning and deep learning approaches for Alzheimer's detection, identifying trends, gaps, and opportunities that guide the design of the proposed model.

CHAPTER 2: LITERATURE REVIEW

In the last decade, the research community has focused a large amount of attention on early identification of Alzheimer's Disease (AD), as an early diagnosis would allow for early therapeutic interventions that could improve one's quality of life. Traditional diagnostic techniques, which primarily involve neuropsychological testing coupled with a clinical assessment, are often unable to identify subtle cognitive changes during the initial stages of the disease. As an alternative, machine learning (ML) and deep learning (DL) techniques have emerged in public health, capable of searching for complex patterns in multimodal biomedical data that could aid in promoting early diagnosis of AD.

2.1 REVIEW OF MACHINE LEARNING MODELS FOR ALZHEIMER'S DISEASE

Within the past decade, ML approaches have been used in various studies to classify individuals who are Hippocampus (HC) from an Mild Cognitive Impairment (MCI) and AD group. The main data sources include magnetic resonance imaging (MRI), positron emission tomography (PET), cerebrospinal fluid (CSF) biomarkers, and/or clinical/cognitive data such as the Mini-Mental State Examination (MMSE) and Clinical Dementia Rating (CDR). Within the MRI studies, the analysis across all includes only either a structural imaging data set or a functional imaging data set; however, these data sources provide diverse contributions toward understanding the disease process, progressing through neuroanatomical atrophy patterns using structural imaging and brain metabolic activity using functional imaging. Clinical data demonstrate the eventual progression of cognitive decline relative to HC individuals, but it is often too late to capture an early diagnosis or make a change in prognosis.

This study, utilizing OASIS, investigated the early prediction of Alzheimer's Disease (AD) using multiple machine learning algorithms to increase diagnostic accuracy and reliability. The authors assessed the performance of Decision Tree (DT), Random Forest (RF), Support Vector Machine (SVM), Gradient Boosting (GB), and Voting Classifier models to determine the best method for AD classification. The features used as input were obtained from structural imaging and patient demographics, ultimately separating normal controls from AD cases. Standard metrics of performance Accuracy, Precision, Recall, and F1-score were assessed, with the goal of being thorough in classification performance assessment. Out of the models testing, the Voting Classifier presented the best validation accuracy of 83%, again outperforming the previous works using the same dataset and single classifiers. By merging several weak learners, ensemble models like Random Forest (RF) and Gradient Boosting (GB) improved predictive stability. Effective boundary separation was shown by the Support Vector Machine (SVM), especially for non-linear data distributions. The study also showed that conventional machine learning techniques can successfully support clinical decision-making and achieve high diagnostic accuracy for Alzheimer's disease (AD) when combined with feature optimization and the integration of multiple classifiers. However, in order to improve overall prediction, the authors also contextualize the significance of multimodal integration and deeper feature extraction.[1].

The researchers used patient-reported data from the National Institute on Aging (NIA), United States of America (USA), which included caregiver interview data and baseline visit data from 496 participants, including 227 control subjects and 269 people with memory issues. Their goal was to develop automated models capable of classifying the stages of Alzheimer's disease (AD), thereby enhancing the accuracy, efficiency, and reliability of diagnostic processes.

The researchers implemented various machine learning methods to evaluate their performance: Neural Networks, a Multilayer Perceptron (MLP), Bagging, Decision Tree (DT), Co-Active Neuro-Fuzzy Inference System (CANFIS), and Genetic Algorithms (GA). The CANFIS model achieved the highest classification accuracy, at 99.55%, and significantly outperformed the other methodologies in classifying the severity of AD, mild, moderate, or severe. One notable hybrid framework that successfully captures nonlinear relationships in clinical data is the CANFIS model, which combines fuzzy logic and neural network learning. Additionally, the researchers connected the disease severity classification to 16 possible pharmacotherapeutic and non-pharmacotherapeutic treatments, highlighting its significance in directing clinical management and treatment planning. Overall, the results point to the need for additional validation and scalability across various datasets to strengthen its applicability, while also suggesting that CANFIS's neuro-fuzzy hybrid architecture may improve clinical decision support in Alzheimer's disease (AD) diagnostics [2].

The purpose of this study was to improve the diagnostic precision of Alzheimer's disease (AD) by applying machine learning (ML) models to longitudinal brain MRI data. The study design took into account the fact that conventional techniques for diagnosing AD depend on clinical characteristics and exclusion criteria, have an accuracy rate of roughly 85%, and necessitate post-mortem confirmation. Thus, developing a generalized automated framework for accurately and promptly diagnosing AD was the aim of the study. A thorough picture of each subject's cognitive state was provided by the dataset used to build and test the machine learning models, which included each subject's medical history, demographic information, and MRI-derived features. Six different supervised learning classifiers were tested in total for binary classification, which separates subjects into groups with and without Alzheimer's disease (AD). Of the tested classifiers, the Gradient Boosting (GB) algorithm produced the best classification accuracy (97.58%) while outperforming other classifiers that attempted to identify complex relationships between neuroimaging and clinical variables. The inclusion of demographic and medical data, along with MRI features, increased both the precision and robustness of the classification. The study findings show that ensemble-based learning methods, specifically GB, are effective at managing high-dimensional medical datasets and predicting the progressive nature of a disease. Overall, this method provides a demonstration that ML-based MRI analysis would have the utility as a new, adjunct tool to clinicians' diagnoses, potentially allowing for diagnosis at earlier stages of AD, more objectively and in a timelier manner [5].

In 2020, Khan and Zubair proposed a machine learning-based framework for using cross-sectional MRI data to identify the progression of dementia. The study focused on two main goals: increasing model efficiency and improving diagnostic accuracy through dimensionality reduction techniques. It did this by using cross-sectional functional MRI data to analyze dementia progression. These methods assisted in removing non-essential and redundant features that are frequently present in high-dimensional neuroimaging data. The authors extracted 17 neuroimaging characteristics linked to Alzheimer's disease (AD) from functional MRI scans of participants in different stages of dementia. After reducing features using Principal Component Analysis (PCA) and Linear Discriminant Analysis (LDA), they implemented machine learning classifiers like Support Vector Machine (SVM), Random Forest (RF), and k-Nearest Neighbors (k-NN). Among these, the SVM model combined with PCA achieved the highest performance, attaining an accuracy of approximately 94%, along with strong precision and recall metrics. The authors emphasized that dimensionality reduction not only improves computational efficiency but also helps reduce noise and overfitting, leading to better classifier generalization. Overall, the proposed machine learning-based framework offers a robust and scalable solution for early-stage dementia detection and monitoring disease progression over time. This study demonstrates great potential for use in clinical practice to support diagnostic pipelines for the detection of dementia in patients with emerging cognitive impairments related to a diagnosis of AD [6].

Gopagoni et al. (2020) presented a novel application of machine learning methods for predicting Alzheimer's disease progression in individuals. They researched the integration of clinical and neuroimaging data to generate a predictive model to differentiate the various stages of the Alzheimer disease continuum. The authors disclosed that they utilized preprocessing methods to address cases of missing data, normalization of attributes, and selection of optimal predictors that were important to the prediction of symptoms of Alzheimer's disease. They also analyzed patterns in progress of the disease by employing various supervised learning approaches, such as Support Vector Machine (SVM), Decision Tree (DT), and Random Forest (RF). The Random Forest classifier yielded the highest level of prediction despite its non-linear relationships and interactions of features. They emphasized that the investigators' findings support the synergistic effect of combining clinical parameters and neuroimaging biomarkers prediction performance, and ultimately diagnosis and intervention, in the management of Alzheimer's disease [7].

Similarly, Kishore et al. (2020) conducted a comprehensive study on the detection and analysis of Alzheimer's disease using multiple machine learning algorithms. Their research compared different ML techniques including Naïve Bayes, k-Nearest Neighbors (k-NN), Support Vector Machine (SVM), and Neural Networks to identify the most effective model for Alzheimer's detection. Using brain MRI datasets and cognitive test parameters, the authors performed detailed statistical and performance evaluations. Among all the models, SVM and Neural Network-based approaches achieved the best results, showcasing superior sensitivity and specificity in distinguishing between normal, mild cognitive impairment (MCI), and Alzheimer's subjects. The study concluded that the choice of preprocessing, feature selection, and classifier combination significantly influences diagnostic accuracy, reinforcing the importance of machine learning in advancing automated Alzheimer's disease detection and prognosis [8].

This study aimed at creating an automated machine learning (ML) pipeline for the early diagnosis of Alzheimer's Disease (AD), using MRI data retrieved from the OASIS database, which contained 343 MRI sessions from 150 subjects. A five-stage machine learning process comprising data preprocessing, feature extraction, feature selection, transformation, and classification was used to create this automated machine learning pipeline. Important clinical and cognitive tests, such as the Mini-Mental State Examination (MMSE), were incorporated as input features. In order to better inform the classification of the imaging data, metrics derived from the imaging are combined with examination, CDR (Clinical Dementia Rating), and ASF (Atlas Scaling Factor). As analytical evaluations, the pipeline also evaluated several classifiers, such as Random Forest (RF), Support Vector Machine (SVM), and k-Nearest Neighbors (k-NN). The RF distinguished between normal and AD subjects with the highest classification accuracy among the classifiers. In order to provide an ML framework for the predictive capability and eliminate modelling process noise from high-dimensional imaging data, the study emphasized the inherent value of using feature selection and data transformation. Overall, the study describes the potential of the integrated machine learning framework as a method for assisting in the early diagnosis of AD and as a trustworthy clinical decision-support tool [9].

By examining longitudinal MRI research output on the OASIS dataset, which comprised 343 MRI sessions with 150 subjects with an average age of 77 years, the study sought to understand the influence of patient-related factors on the progression of Alzheimer's disease (AD). The goal was to explore relationships between demographic variables, which included age, gender, education level and socioeconomic status, and AD severity measured by neurological features derived from MRI T1-weighted imaging, normalized whole brain volume (nWBV), estimated total intracranial volume (eTIV), and Atlas Scaling Factor (ASF), and cognitive severity scores indicated by MMSE and CDR. Exploration of the data revealed that gender, education, and socioeconomic status have a great influence in AD development and progression. The statistical analysis indicated significant differences in nWBV between CDR groups (CDR=0, 0.5, and 1; $p<0.01$), indicating significant structural brain changes measured by MRI associated with dementia severity. The study emphasized the importance of identifying outliers and linearity of features in support of better predictive modeling during analysis. Overall, longitudinal MRI in conjunction with demographic and cognitive features is a relatively solid platform to drive ML for predictive modeling AD, and offers further understanding of individual risk and early support for to improve clinical intervention [10].

This research focused on identifying genetic-based early detection of Alzheimer's Disease (AD) developed a pattern matching and scoring framework to find disease-related gene sequences. Recognizing that genetic factors have a crucial role in AD progression, in addition to lifestyle and environmental factors, the authors employed suffix tree-based pattern identification to sequence distinct polymorphic patterns related to disease-causing and disease-resistant Single Nucleotide Polymorphisms (SNP's). A scoring method was proposed to obtain a precise measure of severity for each gene. The features from the scoring method were input appropriately into a Gradient Boosted Decision Tree (GBDT) classifier, which was evaluated on the ADNI benchmark dataset and determined an accuracy score of 94.16%. The genetic-based classifier developed in this study outperformed previously developed classifiers based on genetic research. The use of gene scoring in addition to ensemble learning allowed the framework to efficiently capture complex genetic patterns in linear time, allowing a strong means of delineating between ADc and healthy controls. While this study focused on developing and evaluating a genetic classifier, it demonstrated how genetic biomarkers could be utilized with sophisticated ML classification algorithms to provide early and accurate assessments of AD diagnosis, previously being absent from traditional neuroimaging and clinical assessment approaches [11].

This research explored the use of machine learning methods for early identification of since Alzheimer's Disease (AD) was examined using the OASIS longitudinal MRI dataset. In light of the critical value of early diagnosis that allows for effective treatment of AD, the study investigated a variety of classifiers such as Logistic Regression (LR), Support Vector Machine (SVM), Decision Tree (DT), Random Forest (RF), and AdaBoost for the identification of AD patients. The performance of each method was evaluated using standard performance metrics (accuracy, recall, and AUC). The results indicate that Random Forest and AdaBoost outperformed other models in their accuracy and AUC, while additionally the Random Forest also performed best with recall, meaning sensitivity to identify AD patients. The Decision Tree had slightly lower accuracy, but took the quickest amount of time to compute (68.788 ms) showing efficiency for a quick classification. Lastly, it was also provided a comparison of deep learning methods and their possibilities with traditional ML techniques. In summary, findings suggest that ensemble learning and boosting methods are effective methods for detection of early AD, while balancing the need for accurate prediction methods along with efficient checks for clinical decision-support systems [12].

The current study presented a computer-aided diagnosis system to facilitate early detection of Alzheimer's Disease (AD). This system applied machine learning models to data from the ADNI and OASIS brain imaging datasets, as the training datasets. Various supervised classifiers applying these two methods included Logistic Regression (LR), Support Vector

Machine (SVM), Random Forest (RF) and Linear Discriminant Analysis (LDA) to automatically differentiate AD patients from healthy controls. Logistic Regression and SVM produced the highest accuracies of 99.43% and 99.10%, respectively on the ADNI dataset, followed by Logistic Regression and RF recording the highest accuracies of 84.33 % and 83.92%, respectively on the OASIS dataset. The results indicate the association of dataset quality and size to model performance, whereby larger benchmark datasets like ADNI can produce higher predictive accuracy compared to smaller benchmark datasets like OASIS. In summary, this study demonstrates the feasibility of ML-based approaches to assist with early AD diagnosis providing fast, accurate detection to assist clinicians with timely intervention and reduce mortality risk among the aging population [13].

The current study concentrated on the early identification of Alzheimer's Disease (AD) by applying a variety of machine learning (ML) classifiers to the OASIS dataset. The authors used six different models: Gaussian Naïve Bayes (GaussianNB), Decision Tree (DT), Random Forest (RF), XGBoost, Gradient Boosting, and a Voting Classifier, for predicting the presence of AD in a cohort of elderly subjects. They assessed the different models by computing accuracy, precision, recall, and F1 score - thus providing a full assessment of classification accuracy across methods. They found that the Voting Classifier performed the best overall with a validation accuracy of 96%, signifying a greater trustworthiness in distinguishing AD subjects from healthy individuals. This study notes that ensemble and boosting methods leverage the complementary advantages of each algorithm, improving predictive performance. Overall, these findings suggest that ML approaches for AD may help facilitate timely and accurate diagnoses, hence decreasing disease progression and mortality, while providing clinical support for early intervention methods [14].

This study investigated the application of speech processing and machine learning (ML) based methods to detect Alzheimer's Disease (AD), with a focus on non-imaging and non-invasive detection methods. Given the multi-domain impact of AD on cognitive, emotional, and language processes, the authors created a framework that integrates feature extraction, attribute selection, and classification to differentiate AD patients from healthy controls. The model assessed ML classifiers while refining the number and redundancy of features, with the aim of improving classification accuracy. The proposed approach yielded an overall classification accuracy of 79%, suggestive of non-imaging, non-invasive potential as a diagnostic tool. The authors established that the process of feature engineering and selection are particularly important in speech-based detection of AD, as this ultimately influences classifier performance. Therefore, the findings of this study suggest that ML models using speech-based biomarkers may provide a promising and non-invasive approach to early screening for AD, as a complement to standard imaging methods, which will serve as an accessible way to monitor cognitive decline [15].

This research examined the role of machine learning (ML) and emerging biomarkers in the assessment of Alzheimer's Disease (AD) in a meta-analysis, seeking to overcome limitations associated with conventional models (e.g., cognitive assessment, imaging, cerebrospinal fluid [CSF] sampling), which may be a costly or invasive process. Emerging biomarkers, in particular, provided promise beyond amyloid-β (Aβ42) and tau protein measures, through novel markers of neuronal injury (neurofilament light, NFL), synaptic dysfunction (neurogranin, BACE1, SNAP-25, synaptophysin), neuroinflammation (sTREM2, YKL-40), and metabolic markers (e.g., d-glutamate). Several machine learning algorithms were compared (Support Vector Machine [SVM], Logistic Regression [LR], Random Forest [RF], and Naïve Bayes) to synthesize and amalgamate these multi-modal biomarkers in predictive models to differentiate healthy controls from subjects with AD. Findings in this study indicated that ML combined with profiles of novel biomarkers show promise for improved diagnostic sensitivity and specificity (and potentially predictive capability), while also suggesting a rapid, inexpensive, non-invasive alternative to early diagnosis of AD. This kind of assessment could support outpatient clinical decision-making, where individuals could receive precise, tailored predictions without having to undergo burdensome amounts of imaging or invasive biopsies [17].

This study presented a noninvasive method for Alzheimer's Disease (AD) stage classification through a machine learning (ML) algorithms and microwave S-parameter measurements. Using six antennas around the head, the authors captured brain changes relating to AD in nine human head models of different sizes. The data were processed using multiple ML classifiers for prediction/differentiation of the four stages of AD. The Logistic Regression Algorithm showed the best prediction performance at 98.97%, representing both accuracy and computational speed. This novel method demonstrates the potential for combining ML and noninvasive microwave sensors as a substitute for the conventional MRI and PET scans which have associated costs and inconvenience for patients. The results demonstrate clinical significance; suggesting that the technology could enable the development of real-time monitoring combined with intelligent stage prediction of AD, facilitating quicker strategies for intervention and patient care with a reduced reliance of either invasive or resource-intensive diagnostics [16].

This research was centered on the early detection of Alzheimer's Disease (AD) through blood-based non-amyloid biomarkers combined with machine learning (ML) methods and gave direction to some of the shortcomings of traditional diagnostics based on amyloid. Since amyloid accumulation occurs quite late in the natural history of the disease, the authors utilized Support Vector Machines (SVM) in combination with novel techniques for feature selection to find protein panels that were predictive of early AD. The authors found five candidate biomarker panels, and one key panel of biomarkers (A2M, ApoE, BNP, Eot3, RAGE, and SGOT) provided a signature indicative of the early stages of the disease. When the authors constructed classification models using the biomarker panels, models consistently reported an overall sensitivity of the model > 80%, specificity > 70%, and area under the receiver operating curve (AUC) ≥ 0.80 during the prodromal stages of the AD, with improvements in the AUC noted at later stages. The main conclusions of the study regarding the designed ML techniques indicated that previously published ML models were not performing well on early-stage data and emphasized the need to find pertinent AD biomarkers to improve their predictive accuracy. Overall, these results showed the promise of non-invasive, blood-based biomarkers with ML algorithms for the early detection of AD, providing a less expensive and more accessible alternative to imaging or cerebrospinal fluid-based biomarkers, and possibly providing opportunities for clinicians to intervene before irreversible neurological impairment occurs [18].

This investigated the progression of neuromarkers related to Alzheimer's Disease (AD) and Mild Cognitive Impairment (MCI), especially in regard to machine learning (ML) applications with data from electroencephalography and magnetoencephalography. The review organized methods based on the type of neuromarker and addressed source reconstruction methods to evaluate their influence on classification performance. Comparison of the MEG-related models indicated exceptional performance on identifying MCI from healthy controls, with classification accuracy well into the 98% percentile. Meanwhile, Electroencephalography (EEG) related models performed similarly for identifying AD from healthy individuals, with very similar accuracies, also approximately 98%. The review emphasized the impact of confounding factors particularly feature extraction, data preprocessing, and the choice of machine learning algorithms noting that these elements are crucial for ensuring model generalizability and effective clinical application within the intended context of use. Overall, it concluded that EEG and Magnetoencephalography (MEG) neuromarkers, when combined with machine learning techniques, offer highly accurate and non-invasive approaches for the detection and monitoring of Alzheimer's disease (AD) and mild cognitive impairment (MCI). However, the review also underscored the need for careful consideration of modeling strategies and experimental design to ensure the development of robust and clinically reliable models.[19].

This study focused on the detection of Alzheimer's disease (AD) using MRI data through two machine learning (ML) approaches designed to capture subtle brain alterations associated with mild cognitive impairment (MCI). In the first approach, MRI scans were denoised and corrected using a 3×3 non-linear filter, followed by k-means segmentation to distinguish white matter and gray matter regions. A Convolutional Neural Network (CNN) was subsequently employed to identify minute structural changes indicative of AD. The second approach utilized Principal Component Analysis (PCA) for feature reduction, isolating white matter, gray matter, and cerebrospinal fluid as key discriminative features, which were then classified using a Multilayer Perceptron (MLP). The study analyzed 602 MRI scans from the ADNI database, comprising both cognitively normal individuals and patients diagnosed with AD. Results demonstrated that PCA-based feature extraction substantially enhanced classification accuracy while reducing processing time, indicating that dimensionality reduction techniques can effectively highlight critical brain structures and improve the efficiency and precision of AD detection.

This study shows that feature engineering can effectively be combined with ML algorithms, such as CNNs or MLPs, to identify the early and intermediate stages of AD, which could allow for a computationally efficient framework for neuroimaging-based diagnosis [20].

This study proposed a framework for neuroimaging-based diagnosis and explored the application of data mining techniques for classification and risk factor analysis of Alzheimer's disease (AD) and Parkinson's disease (PD). A dataset of 487 patients from the Alzheimer's Disease Research Center (ADRC), USA, was used in the study; of these, about 65% had been diagnosed with AD and 40% with PD. Finding the most significant risk factors causing these neurodegenerative diseases was the main goal. The study chose the most pertinent features for model training by combining a ranker search method with attribute evaluation schemes. These chosen features were then used to train a variety of neural network (NN) and machine learning (ML) classifiers to categorize the occurrence of diseases. According to the analysis, age, smoking, diabetes, and genetics were the main risk factors for AD, whereas age, stroke, genetics, and diabetes were the main risk factors for PD.

In general, the results show that data mining can improve knowledge of disease aetiology, facilitate more precise prediction, and aid in the early detection and prevention of neurodegenerative diseases when combined with feature selection and ML-based modelling [21].

In order to improve the classification performance of conventional single machine learning (ML) algorithms, this study concentrated on the early detection of Alzheimer's disease (AD) through the use of ensemble learning. Three target classes Cognitively Normal (CN), Mild Cognitive Impairment (MCI), and AD were created using the ADNI clinical dataset. Then, using ensemble techniques for bagging, boosting, and stacking, patients were categorized according to their clinical and cognitive characteristics. The results show that ensemble methods were superior to individual ML algorithms, as AdaBoost (boosting) achieved the best classification accuracy of 92.7%, an increase of 3.2% to 7.2% from individual classifiers. The study shows that multiple classifiers using ensemble learning can capture complex patterns in clinical data, improving early AD detection and allowing for timely treatment to prevent further cognitive decline [22].

Four significant studies that used machine learning (ML) as a technique for early Alzheimer's disease (AD) detection have been compiled in this review, which also highlights the possible benefits of multimodal data. The first study highlighted the significance of behavioral data and proposed that integrating cognitive and neuropsychological tests increased predictive accuracy. In order to ascertain the onset of AD, the second study investigated neuroimaging analysis and applied machine learning to find the first structural alteration linked to AD. The third study used machine learning (ML) to interpret AD risk factors, found significant variables influencing AD development, and emphasized the need for more research employing more thorough data approaches to better target clinical risk prediction. Finally, the fourth study employed a soft voting ensemble classifier to aggregate multiple models via averaging to improve classification accuracy. These studies indicate that machine learning, particularly when assessed alongside multimodal data and factors, will be a promising improvement in the diagnosis of AD during the early stages of the disease that may lead to actionable interventions and improved health outcomes for patients [23].

This study established an early diagnosis model for Alzheimer's Disease (AD) utilizing non-invasive plasma lipid peroxidation biomarkers. Given the limitations of traditional diagnosis, which is frequently expensive, non-specific, or invasive, the study sought to identify biological markers associated with early AD. To evaluate the diagnostic qualities of six lipid peroxidation compounds that were quantified using a suitable and approved technique, well-characterized subject groups were enlisted. The quantified lipid peroxidation markers were then used to train an elastic-net-penalized logistic regression model to estimate prediction statistics for the outcome. The final model showed excellent calibration properties within acceptable margins of deviation from observed probabilities and good statistical diagnostic test performance (apparent AUC-ROC of 0.883, bootstrap validated AUC-ROC of 0.817). According to the results of this study, plasma lipid peroxidation may be a reliable and non-invasive indicator of early AD; however, there is still a chance to create readily available risk indicators with plasma lipid peroxidation markers to alert fish doctors to possible interference or disruption in regular brain activity [24].

In a Brazilian cohort, the current study investigated the potential of cerebrospinal fluid (CSF) biomarkers for the diagnosis and progression of Alzheimer's disease (AD).We assessed CSF concentrations of amyloid-beta peptide (Aβ1–42), total tau (T-tau), and phosphorylated tau (P-tau, 181Thr) level in 184 elder adults, including AD patients, mild cognitive impairment (MCI) patients, other cognitive impairment patients without AD, and healthy controls. Laboratory-specific cutoffs were established to dissociate patients with AD from controls for Aβ1–42 <416.0 pg/mL (sensitivity 83%, specificity 70%), T-tau levels >76.7 pg/mL (SE 82%, SP 67%), P-tau levels >36.1 pg/mL (SE 83%, SP 49%), and ratios of Aβ1–42/P-tau < 9.53 and Aβ1–42/T-tau < 4.13, which were associated with higher levels of predictive performance (sensitivity and specificity ~78-80%). Moreover, Aβ1–42 < 416.5 pg/mL combined with Aβ1–42/P-tau < 9.5 predicted those with a conversion to dementia within 2 years (hazard ratio 7.24, P = .002). These results corroborate global findings in the field of AD biomarkers, but support the fact that cutoff values are laboratory-specific and suggest that practices will need to address local cutoffs in clinical practice. The current study supports the value of using CSF biomarkers in both the early diagnosis and prognosis of AD [25].

Table 2.1 Machine learning based alzheimer's disease detection

S. No	Method / Technique	Features / Biomarkers	Performance Metrics	Key Findings
1	Decision Tree, Random Forest, SVM, Gradient Boosting, Voting Classifier	MRI images, clinical scores	Accuracy: 83%; Precision, Recall, F1-score reported	Voting classifier showed highest performance; ML methods useful for early AD detection
2	Neural Networks, Multilayer Perceptron, Bagging, Decision Tree, CANFIS, Genetic Algorithms	Clinical and interview data	CANFIS Accuracy: 99.55%	CANFIS outperformed other classifiers; results useful for treatment planning
3	Supervised ML classifiers (Gradient Boosting, etc.)	MRI + Demographic data	Accuracy: 97.58%	Gradient Boosting best for AD vs non-AD classification; supports early detection
4	Dimensionality Reduction + ML	MRI features	–	Feature reduction improved model efficiency for dementia progression detection
5	ML strategies	Clinical data	–	ML effectively predicts AD progression; enhances early detection

6	Random Forest pipeline with data transformation and feature selection	MRI + MMSE, CDR, ASF	Random Forest highest accuracy	Multi-stage pipeline improved classification; combined MRI and clinical scores
7	Exploratory Data Analysis (EDA) + MRI features	MRI + MMSE, CDR, eTIV, nWBV, ASF	–	Gender, education, and socioeconomic status (SES) significantly correlated with AD severity
8	Gradient Boosted Decision Tree with gene scoring	Genetic sequences, SNPs	Accuracy: 94.16%	Gene-based scoring enhanced AD vs healthy classification; efficient linear-time algorithm
9	GaussianNB, Decision Tree, Random Forest, XGBoost, Gradient Boosting, Voting Classifier	MRI + clinical features	Accuracy: Voting Classifier 96%	Ensemble voting classifier improved predictive accuracy; reduces AD mortality
10	Speech processing + ML	Speech features	Accuracy: 79%	Non-invasive speech-based detection; feature selection crucial for performance
11	Elastic-net-penalized Logistic Regression	Plasma lipid peroxidation biomarkers (6 compounds)	AUC: 0.883 (apparent), 0.817 (bootstrap)	Non-invasive early AD diagnostic model; reliable probability predictions

12	CSF biomarkers + statistical analysis	Aβ1–42, T-tau, P-tau, Aβ1–42/P-tau, Aβ1–42/T-tau	Sensitivity: 74–88%; Specificity: 49–80%	Lab-specific cutoffs established for diagnosis and 2-year progression prediction
13	ML with S-parameter data + Logistic Regression	Non-invasive microwave measurements	Accuracy: Logistic Regression 98.97%	Efficient differentiation of 4 AD stages; potential clinical application
14	Ensemble ML: Bagging, Boosting (AdaBoost), Stacking	Clinical data	Accuracy: AdaBoost 92.7%	Ensemble methods outperformed single classifiers; boosting improved early AD detection
15	ML combining cognitive, neuropsychological, risk factor, and ensemble (soft voting)	Cognitive, neuropsychological, risk variables	–	Combining multimodal data with ensemble ML improved recognition; supports therapeutic planning
16	Elastic-net logistic regression	Plasma lipid peroxidation biomarkers	AUC: 0.817–0.883	Six biomarkers used for early AD probability estimation; non-invasive and cost-effective
17	CSF biomarkers, statistical modeling (Cox regression)	Aβ1–42, T-tau, P-tau, Aβ1–42/P-tau, Aβ1–42/T-tau	Sensitivity: 74–88%; Specificity: 49–80%; HR: 7.24	Cutoff values established for AD diagnosis and predicting progression to dementia

2.2 REVIEW OF DEEP LEARNING AND MULTIMODAL FRAMEWORKS

Recent progress in deep learning techniques have allowed for more accurate and automated detection of Alzheimer's disease (AD) using neuroimaging data. For example, a study used a fine-tuned EfficientNet-B5 convolutional neural network (CNN) to analyze MRI scans for early detection of AD. The model was trained on the publicly available augment MRI dataset, which allowed for early detection by detecting subtle characteristics and abnormalities in brain structures corresponding with AD. The system attained an accuracy of 96.64% and demonstrated proficiency and distinguished accuracy by utilizing the landmark capacity of deep CNNs for hierarchical feature extraction. These findings suggest that deep learning approaches hold significant promise to facilitate better early detection and clinical management of AD. In addition, deep learning techniques may provide a non-invasive, low-cost, and powerful option for improving AD patient outcomes [26].

Alzheimer's disease (AD) is a progressive neurological disease that slows memory, reasoning, and behavior, usually in individuals older than 40. Traditional diagnosis and evaluation of AD consist of manual evaluation of magnetic resonance imaging (MRI) data and neuropsychological testing, and is time-consuming and subjective.

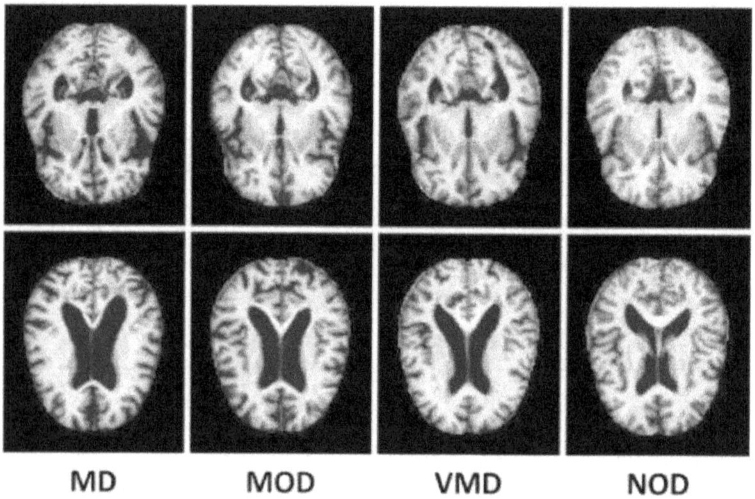

Figure 2.1 AD dataset

Deep Learning (DL) has improved medical imaging analysis with automated and highly accurate methods of evaluation. In this work, we designed a new Convolutional Neural Network (CNN) architectural design called the Alzheimer's Disease Detection Network (ADD-Net) to classify AD stages efficiently. Given the architecture of the model with relatively fewer parameters, the model is suitable for smaller datasets, and synthetic oversampling was utilized to alleviate class imbalance in the MRI images. In comparison to DenseNet169, VGG19, and InceptionResNet V2, ADD-Net achieved an accuracy of 98.63%, an AUC of 99.76%, an F1-score of 98.61%, precision of 98.63%, recall of 98.58% and loss of 0.0549%. These results proved that the model was robust and was able to effectively and accurately identify the early stages of AD, which can provide clinical evaluation or research use [27].

Alzheimer's disease (AD), which is predominant among people aged 60 and older, is the most common form of dementia and a diagnostic dilemma in the early stage of the disease. Identifying mild stage AD is important because the early-mild stage can progress to very mild stage dementia to severe cognitive and functional impairment. Recent efforts in the literature have proposed plans to use DL to evaluate and discover subtle changes in brain networks that the previous literature may have overlooked. In this research project, two MR datasets containing 6400 and 6330 images were used to develop a methodology for identifying mild stage AD. The researchers developed a neural network classifier using VGG16 feature extraction of the MR images to determine the different stages of AD. The model achieved an accuracy of 90.4 and 71.1, precision of 0.905 and 0.71, recall of 0.904 and 0.711, area-under-the-curve (AUC) of 0.969 and 0.85, and F1 score of 0.904 and 0.71 for the datasets. A comparison with previous work suggests this work surpassed the ability to stage AD. These findings provided support for utilizing DL based analysis of MR images as a lower barrier to entry in diagnosing AD in an earlier stage and using results to help guide treatment plans to optimize treatment progression [28].

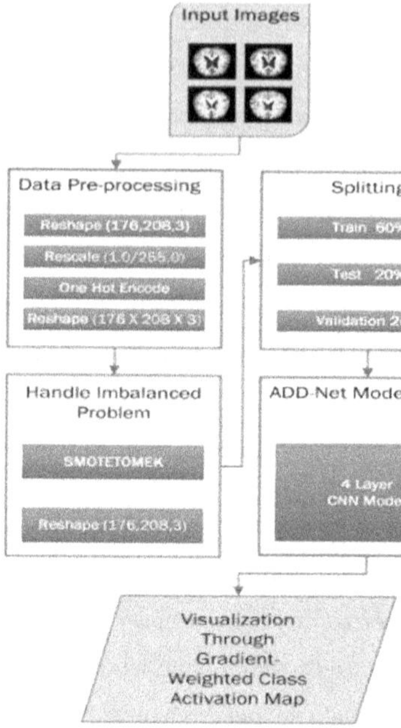

Figure 2.2 ADD-Net architecture [27].

Alzheimer's disease (AD) is the most frequent type of dementia, causing gradual memory declines and decreased ability to carry out daily activities. The early diagnosis of AD is essential in order to facilitate intervention and improve outcomes for the patient in the future. In the last few years, deep learning (DL) algorithms have shown tremendous potential in the analysis of MRI brain scans for the detection of AD. In this investigation, a convolutional neural network (CNN) was carried out to classify AD stages using the Alzheimer's Disease Neuroimaging Initiative dataset of 1,512 mild, 2,633 normal, and 2,480 AD images. The CNN model achieved a high level of accuracy at 99%, outperforming prior machine learning models used with the OASIS dataset. Overall, these findings demonstrate that deep learning models are particularly useful when dealing with large-scale medical imaging and represent a powerful option to support radiologists, medical doctors, or caregivers in the early detection and classification of Alzheimer's Disease [29].

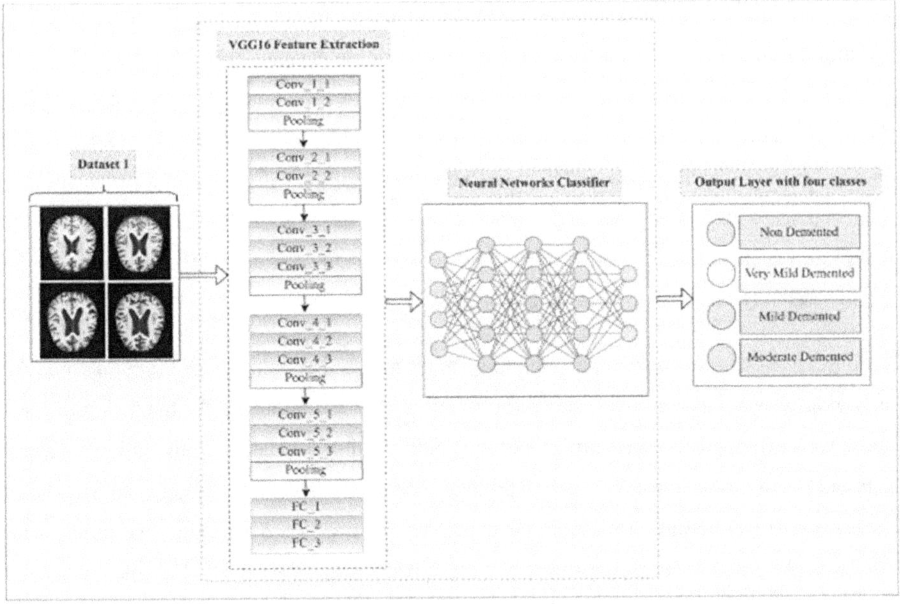

Figure 2.3 VGG16 architecture [28].

Identifying Alzheimer's disease (AD) as early as possible is important for effective preventative treatment and mitigations to disease progression. Traditional analysis methods using MRI typically focus on horizontal-plane scans; however, manuscripts have recently investigated the utility of sagittal MRIs in diagnosing AD. In this study, scans of sagittal MRIs collected from the ADNI and OASIS datasets were leveraged to train deep learning models using transfer learning (TL) methods. Results suggested that sagittal MRIs are equivalent in identifying AD damage but more importantly, identifying early-stage AD than horizontal-plane MRIs. The model development also indicated an important benefit of TL, suggesting that contributions can be made to accurate model development with only limited training datasets. These findings highlight that less commonly utilized MRI planes should be paired with TL based DL methods for improved identification at early disease stages while reducing reliance on large training datasets making this a useful model in clinical applications [30].

AD stages from mild to severe disease. Traditional diagnostic approaches, including medical history, neuropsychological tests, and MRI, often lack sufficient sensitivity and exactness. Recent studies have incorporated deep learning (DL) networks to automatically identify AD patterns identified from MRI data. In the study presented in this paper, a pre-processing step was introduced to improve classification accuracies prior to designing the DL model. The work used the ADNI database and incorporated Haralick features, Local Binary Pattern (LBP) feature extraction, Artificial Neural Networks (ANN), and VGG-19 models. The experimental findings showed that the proposed DL approach was superior to existing approaches, achieving enhanced sensitivity, precision, and overall diagnostic accuracy. This work underscores the benefit of enhanced feature extraction and pre-processing to provide significant improvement to DL-based AD detection systems [31].

A progressive cognitive decline, leading to memory loss and impairment of brain function. An early, non-invasive diagnosis is critical for effective care and treatment for the patient. In this study, we developed a deep learning-based pipeline using a shallow Convolutional Neural Network (CNN) to detect and classify AD stages accurately using 2D T1-weighted MRI brain images. Our pipeline provides global classification (Normal vs. Mild Cognitive Impairment (MCI) vs. AD) and local classification for the further classification of MCI into Very Mild Dementia (VMD), Mild Dementia (MD), and Moderate Dementia (MoD). Testing our model against several state-of-the-art architectures (DenseNet121, ResNet50, VGG16, EfficientNetB7, and InceptionV3), we demonstrated an overall testing accuracy of 99.68% for the AD stage classification. This study demonstrated a robust model required to be interpretable, efficient, and have an output that will provide accuracy to enable precise classification in the detection of AD stages [32].

Early-stage diagnoses allow us to slow its progression and develop strategies for better care. The hippocampus (HC) is one of the first areas of the brain to be affected by AD, and shape and volume are two biomarkers that can be used in early diagnosis. This study proposed a deep learning (DL)-based hippocampus segmentation framework (DL-AHS) which supports automatic segmentation of left and right HC using structural magnetic resonance imaging (MRI). The DL-AHS framework used a U-Net architecture, with two variants: SHPT-Net which involved hyperparameter tuning in U-Net, and RESU-Net which utilized transfer learning from ResNet blocks. Data were processed using MIPAV, and another distinctive augmentation was performed using deep convolutional generative adversarial networks (DC-GANs) in order to enhance model robustness. Results were promising, SHPT-Net was 94.34% accuracy and 93.5% in Dice score; RESU-Net was 97% accuracy and 94% in Dice score. These findings demonstrate the promise of deep learning for accurate hippocampal segmentation and early detection of AD [33].

The majority of present-day studies on Alzheimer's disease (AD) and mild cognitive impairment (MCI) utilize a single data modality to predict outcomes such as AD classification. The combination of multiple data modalities can provide a more complete framework for outcome prediction and analysis in the AD staging analysis. Therefore, we utilize deep learning (DL) methods to collectively analyze imaging (magnetic resonance imaging (MRI)), genetic (single nucleotide polymorphisms (SNPs)), and clinical test data to classify participants into AD, MCI, and controls (CN). In this study, we utilize stacked denoising auto-encoders to extract features from clinical and genetic data, and 3D-convolutional neural networks (CNNs) for imaging data. We also introduce a novel data interpretation method using clustering and perturbation analysis to determine the top-performing features learned by the deep-models. Using the Alzheimer's disease neuroimaging initiative (ADNI) dataset, we show that deep-method prediction models outperform shallow-model prediction methods, which include benchmarks of support vector machine, decision tree, random forest, and k-nearest neighbors classifiers. In addition, we show that a multi-modality dataset outperforms the single-modality model across accuracy, precision, recall, and meanF1 scores. Our models matched findings in the AD literature by identifying the most distinctive features in the hippocampus and amygdala brain regions as well as the Rey Auditory Verbal Learning Test (RAVLT) [34].

Diagnostic techniques that use deep learning algorithms to analyze medical imaging have been developed in the past ten years, especially for the detection of Alzheimer's disease (AD). AD is the seventh leading cause of death worldwide and a major contributor to dementia in general. Since there is currently no cure for AD, early detection is crucial for successful interventions. Using 35 Convolutional Neural Network (CNN) architectures, the research conducted for this study classified brain MRIs into three categories: normal, mild cognitive impairment (MCI), and Alzheimer's disease. A thorough assessment of the effectiveness of 29 distinct pre-trained models was conducted on a total of 2182 MRI images. Performance was better with EfficientNet models than with the others. The EfficientNetB3 model outperformed the others, achieving a 92.98% overall accuracy, 89.78% efficiency for MCI, 94.42% efficiency for AD stage detection, and 97.28% specificity for the AD class. According to the results, the application of EfficientNet models offers a strong and trustworthy classification of AD stage, facilitating early detection and aiding in the classification of preventive clinical interventions [35].

Early diagnosis is particularly important to prevent irreversible damage and improve patient care, even though there are clinically approved pharmaceutical agents that can slow the disease's progression. This study proposes a transfer learning model based on EfficientNetB7, leveraging a pre-trained network architecture for compound scaling to gradually optimize the depth, width, and resolution of the network together. Compared to other pre-trained models such as VGG19 and InceptionV3, EfficientNetB7 has a lower computational complexity, a shorter training and inference times, and a potential for reduced overfitting to achieve a similar performance. Evaluated on the ADNI dataset, this study reports noteworthy results for multi-class classification of AD stages with reported accuracy of 98.2%, sensitivity of 98.08%, specificity of 98%, and F-score of 98.95%. These findings provide evidence for the capability of EfficientNetB7 in accurately detecting an stage stratification of Alzheimer's disease [36].

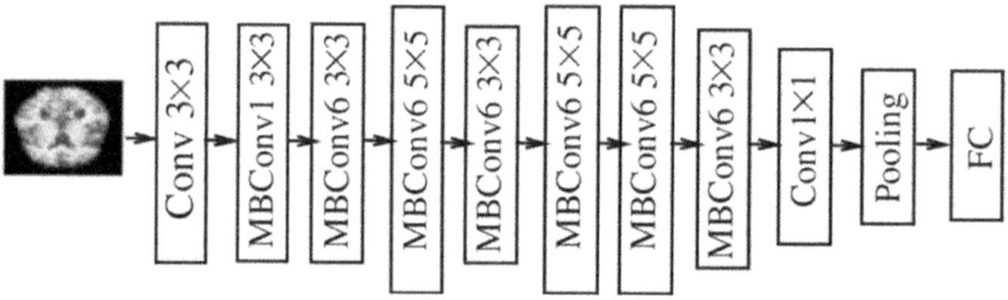

Figure 2.4: Efficient-B7 architecture [36].

Most recent research on Alzheimer's disease (AD) and mild cognitive impairment (MCI) has leveraged a single modality, such as neuroimaging, to predict and stage the disease. A multi-modality approach can help provide a better understanding of the disease progression and classification performance. Herein lies the use of deep learning (DL) methods that analyze and classify multiple data modalities, imaging (MRI), genetics (SNPs) and clinical test scores, to classify patients as AD, MCI or cognitively normal (CN). Stacked denoising auto-encoders were used for feature extraction with clinical and genetic data and 3D convolutional neural networks (CNNs) were used for the imaging data. A new method for interpretation of the data was included to identify top performing features through clustering and perturbation analysis.

The approach was applied to the ADNI dataset and the results showed that deep models out-performed shallow models, which included support vector machines, decision trees, random forest and k-nearest neighbors. Additionally, in the majority of performance metrics, including accuracy, precision, recall, and mean F1-scores, combining multi-modality data outperformed single modality data. The hippocampus, amygdala, and Rey Auditory Verbal Learning Test (RAVLT) scores were among the top features that were identified; these scores were in line with previous AD research and demonstrated the biological significance of the combined features [33].

For AD patients to live as long as possible and receive timely interventions, early detection is essential. Magnetic resonance imaging (MRI)-based machine learning (ML) techniques have been used more and more in clinical practice to speed up AD diagnosis and support clinical decision-making. However, the majority of traditional machine learning techniques for diagnosing AD rely on handcrafted features, which are frequently intricate and necessitate the assistance of experts. To address this limitation, deep learning (DL) models can function as automatic feature extractors, thereby minimizing manual methods while enhancing accuracy. In this context, a pre-trained ResNet50 convolutional neural network (CNN) was suggested to autonomously extract features from MRI for the diagnosis of Alzheimer's disease (AD). We used classifiers like the traditional Softmax, Support Vector Machine (SVM), and Random Forest (RF) classifiers to test this work and compare it to other cutting-edge methods. The proposed ResNet50-based methods exhibited superior classification performance relative to other state-of-the-art mediated models, achieving accuracy values between 85.7% and 99% for MRI ADNI datasets [37].

Recent studies indicate that Alzheimer's disease (AD) can exist for several years before a dementia diagnosis, underscoring the necessity of early intervention. Due to progress in finding biomarkers and getting access to large amounts of medical data, we need powerful computers to make accurate early diagnoses. To achieve this objective, deep learning (DL) frameworks based on convolutional neural networks (CNNs) have been suggested. We created a complete four-step pipeline for finding and staging AD. The steps are (I) preprocessing and preparing the data, (II) adding more data, (III) cross-validation, and (IV) classification and feature extraction. We applied two methods: a simple CNN architecture, and a fine-tuned VGG16 model pre-trained on ImageNet and transferred to medical datasets. Significant improvements in AD classification performance were observed when the models were assessed using seven performance metrics. Across all AD stages, the CNN's accuracy was 99.95% and 99.99%, while the optimized VGG16's accuracy was 97.44%. These results show that DL-based frameworks are especially suitable for early-stage AD detection and can provide better diagnostic performance with less memory usage, overfitting, computational complexity, and required labeled training data [38].

In an effort to improve the classification of Alzheimer's disease (AD) stages, recent studies have developed a Deep Convolutional Neural Network (DCNN) framework that classifies AD stages using brain MRI scans. People have been classified as Normal Controls (NC), Mild Cognitive Impairment (MCI), or AD by the multiclass DCNN classifier. Regardless of the train-test split, the classifier demonstrated exceptional performance with average accuracies of 100% for AD/NC, 92.93% for NC/MCI, and 99.21% for AD/MCI, which translated to a three-class accuracy of 93.86% for all classes. The classifier was trained and tested using the ADNI dataset. The system's robustness was validated by Confusion Matrix (CM) performance testing and Receiver Operating Characteristics (ROC) analysis, which yielded AUCs of 1, 1, and 0.989 for AD, NC, and MCI, respectively. In conclusion, DCNN-based methods resulted in the best discrimination ability and exceeded the accuracy of many previously reported studies for the diagnosis of AD, demonstrating the role of deep learning models for early and accurate staging of neurodegenerative progression [39].

The importance of electroencephalography (EEG) in the early diagnosis and staging of Alzheimer's disease (AD) has also been studied, in addition to the imaging methods already discussed. In one study, features from EEG signals were extracted using a nonlinear multi-band analysis with the Wavelet Packet Transform in order to classify subjects using traditional Machine Learning (ML) and Deep Learning (DL) models. Classifying participants into four groups control (C), mild cognitive impairment (MCI), mild/moderate Alzheimer Dementia (ADM), and Advanced AD (ADA) was the study's goal. In terms of performance, classification accuracies for binary classifications were between 78.9% (C vs. MCI) and 93.8% (MCI vs. ADA) with an accuracy of 56.8% for the multiclass "All vs. All" classification. Notably, for MCI vs. ADM classification, the method improved performance by ~2% compared to earlier algorithms on the same dataset, which these opportunities and relating to the central and parietal brain regions potentials, indicating relative differences in between the levels of pathology associated in AD brought about in the MCI and ADM population. Overall, these results indicate that EEG based feature extraction and classification is another method on par with imaging to be used for early, non-invasive detection of AD [40].

With the growing use of computer-aided detection (CAD), special emphasis has been placed on the classification of brain disease, specifically Alzheimer's disease (AD), primarily since it continues to be one of the most common forms of dementia and can result in fatal outcomes in individuals afflicted with later stages. Although imaging modalities such as MRI, PET, and Computed Topography (CT) scans are frequently used for diagnostic procedures, they overwhelmingly rely on an expert for interpretation. Since detection of AD by using CAD and AI continues to be explored, recent studies have begun to take advantage of pre-processing techniques on MRI images, such as selective clipping, conversion to a grayscale image, and histogram equalization that enhances clarifying visual features and reduces computational burden in support of computer-aided detection of AD. Pre-processing was incorporated prior to classifier development, and machine learning and deep learning models, including the Random Forest Algorithm, XGBoost, and Convolutional Neural Network (CNN), were then implemented for classification. After converting the 4D images created by the ADNI dataset to 2D images and ultimately evaluating detection by the methodology proposed achieved accuracy of 97.57% and sensitivity of 97.60%, ultimately outpacing previously developed and evaluated designs. This study is intended to emphasize the critical role of pre-processing for improving model performance in AD and the impact of high-quality prepared MRI images in classification efficiencies [41].

Automatic segmentation of brain subregions, including Grey Matter (GM), White Matter (WM), Corpus Callosum (CC), and Hippocampus (HC), is a difficult but important first step in diagnosing Alzheimer's disease (AD) because of the structural differences across individuals. Nature-inspired optimization algorithms have been used to tackle this issue. Examples of these nature-inspired optimization algorithms are Genetic Algorithm (GA), Particle Swarm Optimization (PSO), Grey Wolf Optimization (GWO), and Cuckoo Search (CS). Of these algorithms GWO outperforms the others in selecting the best segmentation solution. The regions that have been segmented were validated based on the ground truth (GT) images and the segmented regions achieved a 98% similarity metric. The segmented subregions were then classified using a deep learning classifier, which produced a 95% classification accuracy overall and the HC outperformed the others on every metric with 95% accuracy, 95% sensitivity, and 94% specificity after performing the task with the deep learning classifier.

Finally, the predicted classifications were verified clinically against the Mini-Mental State Examination (MMSE) which proved correlation between the automated predictions. Overall, this study demonstrates the potential that the HC holds as a structural region for diagnosing AD and provides proof of the effectiveness of combining optimization-based segmentation and deep learning classifier metrics [42].

A standard imaging techniques like CT, MRI, and PET are commonly used to assist in diagnosis, but they are often time-consuming, less practical in the early stages, and lack convenience. To eliminate these disadvantages, hybrid deep learning (DL) and machine learning (ML) models are created that will lessen the amount of human intervention is needed, reduce the computational load, and decrease the time-consuming nature of prediction, while also still being accurate. Elaborating on the approach, a hybrid AI model is proposed that combined transfer learning (TL) and permutation-based ML voting classifiers. The first stage of the model extracted features using DenseNet-121 and DenseNet-201, followed by three different ML classifiers- an SVM, Naïve Bayes and XGBoost- in the classification stage, wherein the final decision was made using a voting structure. The model obtained 91.75% accuracy, 96.5% specificity, and 90.25% F1-score and outperformed state-of-the-art existing approaches compared. These results show the promise of hybrid TL-ML approaches in predicting AD diagnosis for MRI images in an early and effective manner, providing an opportunity for practical use in real-world clinical settings [43].

AD primarily results in progressive loss of memory and cognitive function while being the third leading cause of mortality worldwide, following heart disease and cancers. Detecting AD early in the disease process (e.g., Patients with Mild Cognitive decline) remains an important yet challenging task. Structural Magnetic Resonance Imaging (MRI) has been widely studied to help in diagnosing AD versus healthy populations, and deep learning (DL) algorithms have been applied in automated classification of the MRI data. In addition to MRI classification algorithms, Electronic Health Records (EHR) and Single Nucleotide Polymorphism (SNP) datasets have been incorporated in detection of AD as well. In addition, feature selection algorithms have been utilized as part of the machine learning pipeline to find the best subset of input features, minimizing redundancy and improving model performance. Evaluation of model predictions using accuracy, sensitivity, specificity, and multi-class AUC demonstrated that the proposed method achieves a high predictive accuracy for diagnosing AD, and has a reliable training and validation loss, and overall suitability for early and accurate diagnosis for Alzheimer's Disease [44].

Recently, illnesses have been contended with by studying the usage of various deep learning (DL) models to extract the complex patterns in MRI scans to determine the most accurate classifications of AD. In this article we offer a DL-architecture agnostic, computationally efficient ensemble, titled Deep Transfer Ensemble (DTE). The DTE utilizes transfer learning, relied upon by a plethora of deep neural networks and their respective benefits (i.e., hyperparameter randomization), and combines them to provide a pertinent improvement via utilizing differing locally optimum solutions. On large datasets, the DTE achieved extreme classification accuracy with 99.05% and 85.27% accuracy for cognitively normal (NC) vs AD classification, and 98.71% and 83.11% accuracy for mild cognitive impairment (MCI) vs AD classification across two independent and separate splits. Moreover, the measures provided good performance with a small dataset with just 50 samples per class with a maximum accuracy ranging to 85% for NC vs AD. When compared to snapshot ensembles and several other state-of-the-art deep-models on the same dataset, the DTE outperformed the existing method and evaluation cold indicate a strong reliance of the proposed method providing robust and generalized measures and methodologies for a clinically salient utility for early and accurate AD diagnostic components [45].

The current study presents a hybrid AI-based framework composed of a traditional machine learning (ML) genetic analysis and deep learning (DL) medical imaging framework to facilitate accurate diagnosis and staging of Alzheimer's disease. Specifically, machine learning methods Random Forest and Support Vector Machines (SVM) are used to identify genetic variants associated with AD, while deep learning frameworks Convolutional Neural Networks (CNN) and VGG19 are used to analyze image scans (MRI or PET) of the brain to categorize and differentiate stages of dementia. Genetics in tandem with imaging offers a comprehensive and accurate diagnostic platform, surpassing traditional methods of diagnostics. The design of the platform will lessen the dependence of the assessment on expert level knowledge, while providing prospective faster, cheaper, and objective analytics. Overall, this hybrid framework will assist with risk and early detection of AD, continuous assessment, and patient-specific treatment plans and eventually enhance HCPS management of Alzheimer's disease cases [46].

A study introduces a unique deep learning (AD-DL) approach to early detection of AD based on MRI brain images. The approach utilizes three main stages: image pre-processing, training of a deep learning model, and assessing its performance. Five different deep learning models were analyzed for autonomous feature extraction and binary classification, separated into two groupings - without data augmentation (without-Aug,) indicated a CNN-without-AUG, and with data augmentation (with-Aug), indicated the grouping of CNNs-with-Aug, CNNs-LSTM-with-Aug, CNNs-SVM-with-Aug, and transfer learning of VGG16-SVM-with-Aug. An important goal of the analysis attempted to analyze the performance of each model to determine the best performing model in terms of identifying AD, while reviewing performance metrics of accuracy, precision, recall, F1-score, training time, and testing time. The most promising experimental findings demonstrated that the CNN-LSTM with augmentation outperformed the remaining models, achieving accuracy of 99.92%. These initial findings represent a promising foundation for future research on deep learning (DL) based automated identification of AD and realized the importance and potential of hybrid architecture and augmentation in the accuracy of the diagnostic procedure [47].

Alzheimer's disease (AD) is a progressive neurological disorder defined by neuronal atrophy, amyloid deposition, and cognitive, behavioral, and psychiatric deficits. Detecting AD early, specifically in the early mild cognitive impairment (EMCI) stage of AD, is difficult due to cosmetic features that distinguish cognitively normal individuals from EMCI individuals. A hybrid deep learning approach has been proposed to classify EMCI by utilizing multimodal imaging (MRI and PET) and neuropsychological test scores. This system applies a Convolutional Neural Network (CNN) with Long Short-Term Memory (LSTM) units that utilizes Adam optimization to update the weights of the LSTM units to optimize classification performance. This technique can achieve 98.5% accuracy in differentiating cognitively normal controls from EMCI patients. This demonstrates the capabilities of deep neural networks to autonomously identify imaging biomarkers and provide early diagnosis techniques for AD. Combined with early diagnosis, patients may be able to receive timely intervention and treatment planning [48].

This research is responding to the issue of detecting Alzheimer's disease (AD) using MRI scans in situations with constrained training data available to train a deep learning model. In the literature, a growing number of published works are documenting the success of transfer learning using 2D convolutional neural networks (CNNs), which entail acquiring a sequence of 2D MRI slices from a 3D MRI volume, and using the pre-trained CNNs to classify each slice independently. However, this method does not allow for the sequential and spatial relationships between slices to be captured. The suggested new approach in this research utilizes a CNN for feature extraction, but adds a recurrent neural network (RNN) to the architecture, which predicts a sequence of slices rather than classifying each slice independently. Making decisions based on all slices in the MRI volume, rather than independent slices, accuracy of the model is improved. The experimental findings presented in this paper demonstrate that the addition of an RNN following the CNN increased the accuracy of the overall system, and emphasizes the importance of sequential modeling for volumetric medical image analysis in diagnosing AD [49].

Recently, deep learning (DL) algorithms have been utilized as strong tools for use in medical image processing and provide necessary assistance to radiologists to diagnose disease accurately. This review discusses the use of DL algorithms to detect Alzheimer's Disease (AD) by performing an evaluation of 103 studies from multiple research databases that utilized specific inclusion criteria. This review focuses specifically on DL algorithms such as convolutional neural networks (CNN), recurrent neural networks (RNN), and transfer learning (TL) that are examined on neuroimaging modalities such as Magnetic Resonance Imaging (MRI) and Positron Emission Tomography (PET). These methods provide DL to enable detection, segmentation, and degree of severity of AD through thorough evaluation of the neuroimaging radiology data. Other studies proposed alternative markers related to the evaluation of AD; however, this review indicates the studies of DL methods that used imaging data. The findings of the analysis indicate important progress in studies utilizing DL methods, but also may inform the need for additional studies utilizing advanced DL methods for tracking the progression from Mild Cognitive Impairment (MCI) to AD [50].

This study explores early detection of AD using supervised machine learning (ML) and deep learning (DL) models, trained with magnetic resonance imaging (MRI) from the Open Access Series of Imaging Studies (OASIS) dataset. Models used for this study included Random Forest and Logistic Regression from traditional ML, Extra Trees from ensemble learning, and a CNN from DL. Each respective model was evaluated in terms of accuracy, precision, recall, and area under the curve (AUC), where the CNN gave the highest accuracy and AUC but Extra Trees gave the highest precision and recall, highlighting that both DL and ensemble learning models can achieve competitive performance for early detection of AD [51].

In recent years, the biomedical field has increasingly started to implement digital image processing and Computer-Aided Diagnosis (CAD) for clinically accurate and efficient assessments. Timely and accurate diagnosis of disease (early-stage detection) is critical to improving quality of life and life expectancy among patients with Alzheimer's Disease (AD). While multimodal analysis approaches have demonstrated superiority over manually run evaluation processes, there are still pricey and inefficient diagnostic procedures in place given the limitations of Magnetic Resonance Imaging (MRI) devices. This study presents a new CAD approach for predicting AD that relies on sophisticated image processing and deep learning methods. MRI images, which are typically noisy from thermal activity associated with hardware, are first restored with a 2D Adaptive Bilateral Filter (2D-ABF) and then enhanced using Adaptive Histogram Adjustment (AHA) to improve brightness and contrast. The Region of Interest (ROI) is segmented using Adaptive Mean Shift Modified Expectation Maximization (AMS-MEM), and feature extractions are completed using the second order of the 2D Gray Level Co-Occurrence Matrix (2D-GLCM). A Deep Convolutional Neural Network (DCNN) is then used to classify stages of AD for effective diagnostic decision-making. The experimental results show that the new methodology provided superior efficacy in comparison to existing systems on basis of accuracy and efficiency [52].

A lightweight Stacked Convolutional Neural Network with a Channel Attention Network (SCCAN) has been suggested for MRI-based AD classification in order to solve this problem. SCCAN accomplishes this by sequentially stacking five CNN modules to form a multi-level, hierarchical feature extraction pipeline that minimizes noise and maximizes the efficacy of each extracted feature. To improve model efficiency, features are extracted, processed, and the most informative features are selected using a channel attention module. Additionally, SCCAN/MSCCAN performs effective classification while drastically lowering the number of parameters needed to train these techniques on smaller datasets. A balanced class distribution of samples was kept for each class in order to rectify the class imbalance in the Kaggle MRI dataset. After conducting extensive experiments of the ADNI1 Complete 1Yr 1.5T, Kaggle, and OASIS-1 datasets, accuracy was achieved at 99.58%, 99.22%, and 99.70% respectively. Overall, the SCCAN model outperformed many state-of-the-art models and is a significant advancement in MRI-based classification of AD [53].

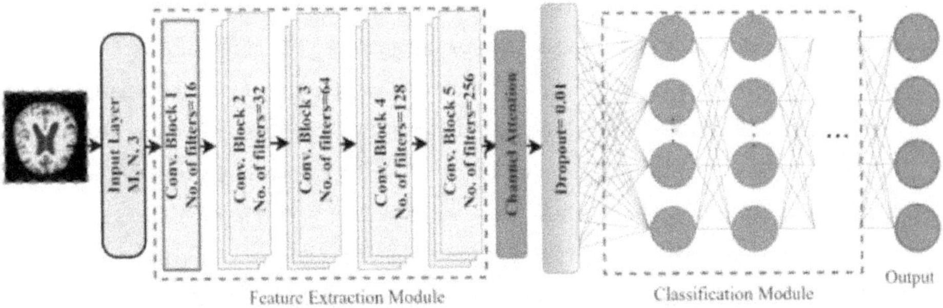

Figure 2.5: SCCAN [53].

A detailed examination of specific regions of the brain using segmented detection of Magnetic Resonance Imaging (MRI) would be necessary for an accurate diagnosis of Alzheimer's disease. The performance of supervised machine learning techniques is frequently below the industry standard, they require human expert involvement, are laborious, complex, and rely on manually extracted features. On the other hand, deep learning (DL) improves training and offers automated feature detection. The Alzheimer Disease (AD) dataset, which has four classes mildly demented, moderately demented, non-demented, and very mildly demented and a recognized class imbalance, is one data type that is frequently used in MRI. In response, the suggested method balanced the dataset and addressed class imbalance by using an adaptive synthetic oversampling technique. The suggested approach in this study integrated VGG16 and EfficientNet-B2 in an ensemble, which gathers predictions from several models to discover increasingly intricate and subtle patterns. To enhance the model's performance, the input and output features from both networks were combined and fed into extra learning framework layers. Based on work with two publicly available datasets, the proposed method shows excellence, earning 97.35% and 99.64% AUC for multiclass classification and 97.09% and 99.59% AUC for binary classification. The suggested approach and procedures perform better than earlier research, raising the bar for early-stage AD diagnosis [54].

Early-stage AD prediction is made more difficult by the variability and inconsistency of traditional diagnostic techniques like blood tests, behavioral assessments, cognitive tests, medical history reviews, and MRI imaging. The current study presents DeepCurvMRI, a convolutional neural network (CNN) framework based on curvelet transform (CT), to improve the accuracy of early-stage AD detection using MRI images in order to get around the aforementioned limitations. Important anatomical features are first extracted from MRI images using CT pre-processing, and these features are then used to train the CNN model. The Alzheimer's MRI dataset from Kaggle was used to test the framework for binary and multi-class classification tasks. With leave-one-group-out (LOGO) cross-validation, DeepCurvMRI obtained a binary classification accuracy of 98.71% ± 0.05, a sensitivity of 99.05% ± 0.10%, a specificity of 98.50% ± 0.03%, and an F1-score of 99.21 ± 0.08. The multi-class accuracy was 98.62% ± 0.10%. Performance was validated through 5-fold cross-validation and randomly stratified 10-fold cross-validation. The outcomes demonstrated superior performance over current methods and demonstrated DeepCurvMRI capacity to detect significant anatomical changes in MRI images and more accurately differentiate between disease stages [55].

Table 2.2 Deep learning and multimodal for AD

Sr. No	Deep Learning/ Multimodel Model	Dataset	Imaging Modality	Task / Classification	Performance Metrics	Key findings
1	VGG16 + Neural Network	MRI (6400 & 6330 images)	MRI	Early AD detection	Accuracy: 90.4%, 71.1%; Precision: 0.905, 0.71; Recall: 0.904, 0.711; AUC: 0.969, 0.85; F1: 0.904, 0.71	Multi-class classification; compared with previous studies
2	CNN	ADNI (Normal: 2633, Mild: 1512, AD: 2480)	MRI	AD stage classification	Accuracy: 99%	Compared with ML methods on OASIS dataset
3	TL (Sagittal MRI)	ADNI & OASIS	MRI (Sagittal)	Early AD detection	Comparable to horizontal-plane MRI	Used Transfer Learning on

						sagittal plane MRI

4	VGG19, LBP, ANN	ADNI	MRI	AD detection	Higher accuracy than classical ML	Included Haralick & LBP feature extraction
5	Shallow CNN	2D T1-weighted MRI	MRI	Normal vs MCI vs AD, and VMD/MD /MoD	Accuracy: 99.68%	Also compared with DenseNet121, ResNet50, EfficientNetB 7, VGG16, InceptionV3
6	U-Net, SHPT-Net & RESU-Net	ADNI & NITRC	Structural MRI	Hippocampus segmentation & AD detection	SHPT-Net: Accuracy 94.34%, DSC 93.5%; RESU-Net: Accuracy 97%, DSC 94%	DC-GAN for augmentation; Left/right HC segmentation
7	EfficientNet B0/B2/B3	ADNI (2182 images)	MRI	Normal / MCI / AD	Accuracy: 92.98%; Precision: 89.78%; Sensitivity: 94.42%; Specificity: 97.28%	Compared 29 pre-trained CNN models

8	EfficientNet B7	ADNI	MRI	Multi-class AD stages	Accuracy: 98.2%; Sensitivity: 98.08%; Specificity: 98%; F1: 98.95%	Transfer Learning; Compound scaling coefficient used
9	3D-CNN + Stacked Denoising Autoencoders	ADNI	MRI + SNP + Clinical	CN / MCI / AD	Multi-modality outperformed single modality (accuracy, precision, recall, mean F1)	Identified hippocampus, amygdala, and RAVLT as top features
10	ResNet50 + SVM/RF/Softmax	ADNI	MRI	AD detection	Accuracy: 85.7%–99%	Automatic feature extraction from MRI
11	CNN / VGG16 TL	Various	MRI	Multi-class AD stage	Accuracy: 99.95% (CNN), 97.44% (VGG16)	Preprocessing, augmentation, transfer learning, cross-validation
12	DCNN	ADNI	MRI	NC / MCI / AD	AD/NC: 100%, NC/MCI: 92.93%, AD/MCI: 99.21%, 3-way avg: 93.86%	ROC and AUC also reported (0.989–1)

13	EEG + ML/DL	EEG signals	EEG	C / MCI / ADM / ADA	Max Acc: 93.8% (MCI vs ADA), 56.8% (all vs all)	Wavelet packet for feature extraction; binary & multi-class
14	CNN + TL + ML Ensemble (DenseNet121, DenseNet201 + SVM/XGBoost/Naïve Bayes)	Kaggle MRI (6200 images)	MRI	Mild / Moderate / Non-demented / Very mild	Accuracy: 91.75%; Specificity: 96.5%; F1: 90.25%	Voting classifier ensemble; permutation based
15	Hybrid CNN + RNN	MRI	MRI	Sequential slice analysis for NC / AD	Improved accuracy over CNN-only	Captures relationships across slices
16	SCCAN (Stacked CNN + Channel Attention)	ADNI1, Kaggle, OASIS-1	MRI	AD classification	Accuracy: 99.58%, 99.22%, 99.70%	Lightweight, reduces parameters, suitable for small datasets
17	Ensemble (VGG16 + EfficientNet-B2)	Kaggle & ADNI	MRI	Multi-class & binary AD	Multi-class Acc: 97.35%, AUC: 99.64%; Binary Acc: 97.09%, AUC: 99.59%	Addressed class imbalance with adaptive synthetic oversampling

18	DeepCurvMRI (Curvelet Transform + CNN)	Kaggle MRI	MRI	Multi-class & binary AD	Multi-class Acc: 98.62%, Sens: 99.05%, Spec: 98.50%, F1: 99.21; Binary Acc: 98.71%	LOGO, 10-fold, 5-fold cross-validation tested

To summarize, deep learning methods have shown great promise in relation to the early detection, staging, and classification of Alzheimer's Disease through myriad imaging modalities, most predominately with MRI. The advent of more complex architectures such as convolutional neural networks, transfer learning models such as VGG and EfficientNet, hybrid convolutional neural network-recurrent neural networks, and ensemble methods, have all positively impacted the diagnostic accuracy, sensitivity, and specificity over conventional machine learning approaches. These methods have been further advanced though multi-modal data, attention mechanisms, and feature extraction improvements to assist in the detection of subtle patterns pertaining to the disease. Challenges including data imbalance, small sample sizes, and interpretation of machine learning models still exist in the clinical forecasting of Alzheimer's Disease. Nevertheless, deep learning, expanded computational capability, and big data keeps driving improvements in automated diagnosis of Alzheimer's Disease early and precise, and ultimately improve patient care and management from this debilitating illness. Overall, this work underpins the use of deep learning through imaging to ultimately transform clinical forecasting of Alzheimer's Disease.

2.3 CRITICAL ANALYSIS OF RESEARCH GAPS

Despite remarkable progress in deep learning (DL) methods for the detection of Alzheimer's Disease (AD), there persist gaps in the field of research. First, the majority of studies have relied significantly on single-modality imaging datasets, mostly in the form of MRI, limiting a more comprehensive quantification of disease progression. Despite their promise, multi-modality approaches that will incorporate genetic, clinical, and imaging data are still not well established in the literature. Second, imbalanced datasets and the lack of large, high-quality annotated datasets are continuing obstacles to the application of deep learning for AD detection particularly for high- capacity DL models which may lead to overfitting. Third, there is insufficient attention to model interpretability and clinical relevance which discourages application by clinicians and healthcare workers who can deploy the models. Fourth, while numerous models report high accuracy, there has yet to crystallize an established and accepted process of comparing performance among models across datasets. Thus, albeit numerous models report high accuracy, it has been difficult to compare direct accuracy among models shared across datasets. Finally, these issues need to be addressed to support the eventual translation of DL models into an easily deployable practical clinical tool to provide early detection and treatment of AD.

1. Dependence on Single-Modality Data

One of the most persistent limitations observed in the literature is the heavy reliance on single-modality imaging datasets, particularly structural Magnetic Resonance Imaging (MRI). While MRI provides detailed information about anatomical brain changes, it does not capture other crucial biomarkers associated with AD, such as metabolic activity, functional connectivity, genetic susceptibility, or cognitive behavior. Studies relying solely on MRI may thus provide a partial and sometimes biased view of disease progression. Multimodal data integration combining MRI, Positron Emission Tomography (PET), Electroencephalography (EEG), genetic information (e.g., APOE genotype), and clinical assessments such as the Mini-Mental State Examination (MMSE) or Clinical Dementia Rating (CDR) is still relatively underexplored. Integrating such heterogeneous data can provide a more holistic understanding of both structural and functional brain deterioration. However, the challenge lies in aligning data across modalities due to differences in scale, noise, dimensionality, and missing values. Future research must therefore focus on robust fusion mechanisms capable of learning from incomplete or imbalanced multimodal data while preserving relevant inter-modality relationships.

2. Data Imbalance and Limited Annotated Datasets

Another major research gap concerns the lack of large, balanced, and well-annotated datasets. Most existing AD datasets, such as ADNI (Alzheimer's Disease Neuroimaging Initiative), OASIS (Open Access Series of Imaging Studies), and Kaggle-based collections, contain a limited number of labeled samples especially for the early or mild cognitive impairment (MCI) stages. These smaller subsets result in highly imbalanced datasets, where the number of non-demented subjects significantly outweighs the demented ones. This imbalance can bias learning algorithms toward majority classes, causing underrepresentation of critical early-stage cases that are most relevant for clinical interventions. Additionally, acquiring high-quality annotated MRI or PET data is expensive, time-consuming, and dependent on expert evaluation, leading to limited accessibility in developing regions. While data augmentation techniques and transfer learning have been introduced to mitigate such issues, they cannot fully substitute for the diversity and heterogeneity of real-world clinical data. Addressing these data challenges will require the establishment of larger, open-access, standardized datasets with harmonized imaging protocols and inclusion of diverse demographic cohorts to enhance model generalizability.

3. Lack of Interpretability and Clinical Trust

A fundamental obstacle in the deployment of DL-based diagnostic models is their lack of interpretability often referred to as the "black-box" problem. Many convolutional and hybrid networks can achieve high predictive accuracy, yet they fail to explain the rationale behind their classifications. Clinicians are therefore hesitant to trust model outputs that cannot justify which features or regions of the brain contributed to the diagnosis. In the medical domain, where ethical responsibility and patient safety are paramount, interpretability is not optional but essential. While Explainable AI (XAI) methods such as Gradient weighted class activation mapping (Grad-CAM), LIME, and SHAP have been introduced, their adoption in AD detection remains inconsistent. Furthermore, many studies limit interpretability to post-hoc visualization rather than integrating it into the training process. There is also a lack of standardized evaluation metrics for measuring interpretability, making it difficult to assess whether an explanation is clinically meaningful. For future research, it is imperative to design self-explainable and attention-based architectures that align AI decision-making with neuropathological understanding bridging the gap between computational reasoning and clinical interpretability.

4. Benchmarking and Reproducibility Issues

Although numerous studies report high accuracy, there is no universally accepted benchmark protocol for evaluating AD detection models. Variations in data preprocessing, train-test splits, augmentation strategies, and evaluation metrics often make it impossible to perform direct comparisons across studies. For instance, one study might use accuracy as a primary measure, while another emphasizes the Area Under the ROC Curve (AUC) or F1-score. Similarly, differences in dataset versions (e.g., ADNI-1 vs. ADNI-2) and preprocessing pipelines (e.g., skull stripping, normalization techniques) can cause substantial performance discrepancies even when identical models are used. These inconsistencies pose challenges to reproducibility and external validity two fundamental pillars of scientific rigour. In the absence of standardized frameworks and transparent reporting, there is a risk of developing models that achieve strong performance on benchmark datasets but fail to generalize effectively in real-world clinical settings. In order to solve this, future studies should place a high priority on reproducibility and transparency by implementing strategies like cross-dataset validation, open-source code sharing, and the development of community-wide benchmarking standards to guarantee impartial and trustworthy model evaluation.

5. Barriers to Clinical Translation and Real-World Deployment

Only a small number of AI systems for Alzheimer's disease (AD) detection have effectively made the leap from lab research to clinical practice, despite significant research advancements. The lack of integration with clinical workflows and inadequate validation on a variety of real-world datasets are the main causes of this gap. Models trained on controlled datasets may perform poorly in novel clinical settings due to the wide variations in medical imaging data across scanners, acquisition protocols, and patient populations.

Furthermore, a lot of research ignores real-world implementation issues like scalability, regulatory compliance, and inference speed. Legal and ethical issues, such as patient privacy, data ownership, and model accountability, present additional difficulties. The secure and ethical integration of AI systems into radiology and neurology workflows in compliance with established regulations like HIPAA and GDPR is frequently overlooked in current research.

Therefore, translating DL-based AD systems into practical diagnostic tools requires multi-institutional collaboration, rigorous clinical trials, and explainable decision-support interfaces that can assist clinicians rather than replace them.

In summary, the research landscape in AI-based Alzheimer's detection, though promising, is still evolving and fragmented. The key gaps include over-reliance on single-modality data, scarcity of annotated and balanced datasets, insufficient focus on model interpretability, inconsistent benchmarking, and limited clinical deployment. Bridging these gaps requires a multidisciplinary approach combining advances in data curation, model design, explainability, and healthcare ethics. Future research must prioritize multimodal fusion frameworks, standardized validation protocols, and clinically explainable models that can serve as reliable, transparent, and deployable diagnostic tools for early Alzheimer's disease detection.

2.4 FUTURE RESEARCH DIRECTIONS IN AI-BASED ALZHEIMER'S DETECTION

Given the rapid advancements in artificial intelligence and medical imaging, several promising research directions emerge for future Alzheimer's detection and progression modeling. First, multimodal fusion frameworks that combine MRI, PET, EEG, genetic, and clinical data should be further developed. Such integrative approaches capture the complex interplay between brain structure, metabolism, and cognitive decline, providing a holistic representation of disease pathology. Second, longitudinal modeling using recurrent and graph-based neural networks can capture temporal changes in brain morphology and cognitive scores, enabling prediction of disease trajectory rather than static classification.

Another critical direction involves the use of federated learning for privacy-preserving model training across multiple hospitals or research institutions. By allowing decentralized training on local data without sharing sensitive information, federated learning addresses privacy concerns while improving model generalization across diverse populations. Similarly, self-supervised and few-shot learning techniques can overcome the challenge of limited labeled data by leveraging large unlabelled datasets for representation learning. These methods are particularly relevant for rare early-stage AD data where annotated examples are scarce.

Standardization and model robustness will be crucial from the standpoint of clinical translation. Due to differences in preprocessing pipelines, dataset sizes, and evaluation protocols, many of the current studies are not reproducible. Research study comparability and trust will be improved by establishing open benchmarks, standardized MRI preprocessing workflows, and explainability reporting guidelines. Furthermore, early screening, ongoing patient monitoring, and individualized treatment planning may be made easier by the incorporation of real-time AI decision support systems into hospital infrastructure.

In conclusion, scalable, interpretable, and morally sound AI systems that integrate multimodal data, protect patient privacy, and yield clinically useful insights should be the focus of future research. These directions hold promise to bridge the current gap between laboratory research and real-world deployment of AI in Alzheimer's care.

2.5 EXPLAINABLE ARTIFICIAL INTELLIGENCE (XAI) AND INTERPRETABILITY IN ALZHEIMER'S DISEASE RESEARCH

While deep learning models have achieved exceptional accuracy in Alzheimer's Disease (AD) detection and classification, their limited interpretability remains a major barrier to clinical adoption. Medical practitioners require not only accurate predictions but also explanations for the model's decisions to ensure clinical trust and accountability. This need has given rise to the field of Explainable Artificial Intelligence (XAI), which focuses on developing transparent and interpretable AI systems that can justify and visualize their outputs in a medically meaningful way.

The goal of XAI techniques in the context of AD diagnostics is to determine how and why a model determines that an MRI scan is suggestive of Alzheimer's disease or a specific stage of dementia. Gradient-weighted Class Activation Mapping (Grad-CAM), Layer-wise Relevance Propagation (LRP), Local Interpretable Model-Agnostic Explanations (LIME), and SHapley Additive explanations (SHAP) are notable XAI techniques. Clinicians can confirm whether the network concentrates on medically relevant areas like the entorhinal cortex, amygdala, or hippocampal regions by using the heatmaps that Grad-CAM and LRP provide, which highlight key brain regions that contribute most to model predictions. However, LIME and SHAP measure how much each prediction is influenced by specific input features, like clinical parameters (e.g., age, education level, or MMSE scores). These methods enable both visual and numerical interpretability, facilitating the integration of AI systems into clinical workflows.

These XAI methods have been used in recent research on multimodal datasets and imaging of Alzheimer's disease. For example, cortical thinning and hippocampus atrophy regions linked to the progression of mild cognitive impairment (MCI) have been identified using Grad-CAM visualizations. According to SHAP-based analyses, the most significant characteristics in predicting cognitive decline are age, memory scores, and gray matter density. Researchers have verified the biological plausibility of deep learning predictions by comparing these AI-derived results with well-established neuropathological evidence, thereby enhancing clinician confidence in automated systems. By automatically weighing the significance of particular features or brain regions during training, attention mechanisms have also been incorporated into architectures such as Vision Transformers (

ViT) and attention-gated CNNs, further enhancing model interpretability.

Notwithstanding the advancements, difficulties still exist. Simplifying a complex model to make it understandable may lessen its predictive power. Interpretability frequently trades off accuracy. Furthermore, if the underlying feature maps are not calibrated correctly, visual explanations may occasionally be deceptive. The absence of consistent evaluation metrics for interpretability is another drawback, which makes it challenging to compare XAI methods across studies in an unbiased manner. Therefore, rather than approaching XAI as a post-hoc analysis, the current research trend seeks to incorporate it into the model architecture itself. By incorporating interpretability into the learning process, this method known as self-explainable deep learning better meets the demands of clinical decision-making.

Interpretability will be a key component of this study's suggested AlzFusionNet framework. While SHAP analysis will be used to rank the significance of clinical variables like MMSE and CDR scores, Grad-CAM will be used to visualize disease-relevant brain areas activated during MRI-based classification. This dual-level interpretability will bridge the gap between algorithmic output and clinical reasoning by enabling the extraction of both radiological and clinical insights from the model. Explainable AI is incorporated into the framework to improve transparency and support a reliable AI ecosystem in neurodiagnostic practice, guaranteeing accurate and interpretable predictions.

Ultimately, explainable AI marks a paradigm shift in Alzheimer’s diagnostics, transforming deep learning models from “black boxes” into “glass boxes.” This integration of performance and interpretability has the potential to revolutionize medical AI systems, making them viable tools for evidence-based, ethically aligned, and clinically accountable decision support in neurodegenerative disease management.

2.6 SUMMARY

This chapter examined deep learning techniques for the detection and classification of Alzheimer's Disease using neuroimaging modalities, and it highlighted specific models, including convolutional neural networks, hybrid CNN-RNN architectures, transfer learning, and ensemble frameworks. The different performance metrics, such as accuracy, sensitivity, specificity, and AUC, indicate that DL models perform generally better than traditional machine learning models in detecting and classifying Alzheimer's Disease. Moreover, the studies suggest a trend towards multi-class classification of AD stage and current advances in multi-class models include attention mechanisms to enhance feature selection. However, obstacles remain such as data scarcity, class imbalance, interpretability, and standardization. Overall, deep learning is deeply effective in promoting early and accurate AD detection, providing for greater advancement of these models in future research to provide for the current obstacles.

CHAPTER 3: MATERIALS AND METHODS

3.1 DATASET DESCRIPTION

For this study, we leveraged longitudinal MRI scans alongside clinical data to investigate Alzheimer's disease (AD) prediction and progression. The primary sources of data were the Open Access Series of Imaging Studies (OASIS) repository, complemented by verified implementations of dementia MRI datasets from Kaggle. These datasets provide a unique combination of imaging and clinical information, which allows for a multimodal approach an essential factor in capturing the complexity of Alzheimer's disease and improving the accuracy of classification models.

Participants in the dataset were divided into two main categories: those diagnosed with Alzheimer's Disease (AD) and those without (Non-AD). The longitudinal structure of the OASIS dataset is particularly valuable, as it includes repeated observations of the same individuals over time. This allows for the analysis of both structural brain changes and cognitive decline as the disease progresses. MRI scans were obtained using standardized imaging protocols to ensure consistency, while the accompanying clinical measures offered insight into cognitive performance and demographic factors, which are critical for understanding individual differences in disease development.

The clinical dataset included several key attributes, encompassing both cognitive assessments and demographic information, as summarized in Table 3.1:

Table 3.1: Clinical Features in the Longitudinal MRI Dataset

Attribute	Description / Purpose

Age	Age of the participant in years, serving as an important demographic predictor for dementia risk.
Gender	Male or Female indicator, reflecting demographic influences on disease prevalence and progression.
Education	Number of years of formal education completed; higher education often correlates with greater cognitive reserve, potentially delaying the onset of symptoms.
Socioeconomic Status (SES)	Composite measure based on income, education, and occupation; lifestyle and environmental factors reflected by SES can impact dementia risk.
Mini-Mental State Examination (MMSE)	Widely used cognitive assessment scoring from 0–30, measuring the severity of cognitive impairment.
Clinical Dementia Rating (CDR)	Standardized dementia staging scale ranging from 0–3, serving as a key reference for disease classification in this study.
Estimated Total Intracranial Volume (eTIV)	Represents total brain size; used for normalization of regional brain volumes to account for individual anatomical differences.
Normalized Whole Brain Volume (nWBV)	Ratio of brain tissue volume to total intracranial volume, reflecting the degree of brain atrophy.
Atlas Scaling Factor (ASF)	Scaling factor derived from registering MRI scans to a standard brain atlas, aiding in volume normalization across participants.

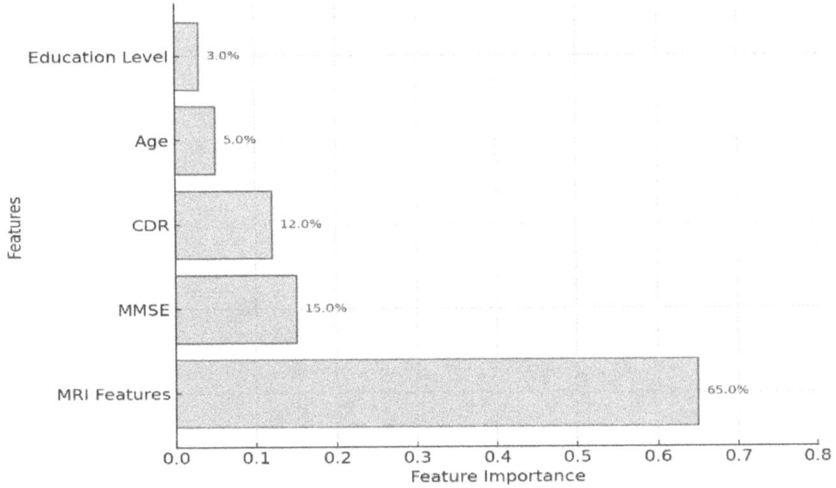

Figure 3.1: Importance feature in AlzFusionNet

In this context, cognitive assessment tools, including the MMSE and CDR, serve as the primary ground-truth biomarkers of disease severity. Morphological assessment tools, including nWBV and eTIV, in other words, the anatomic structure of the brain, can be measured via MRI as evidence of brain atrophy. Demographics (e.g., age, sex, education, and SES) provide context for interpreting heterogeneity in the experience of individuals as they develop the condition and experience decline due to the condition.

MRI data were preprocessed extensively for ensuring consistency across sessions or subjects. The preprocessing involved bias-field correction for intensity inhomogeneities; skull stripping for brain tissue extraction; normalization of intensity; and spatial registration to MNI152. Two-dimensional axial slices were extracted from preprocessed volumes for analysis; the images were 128 × 128 pixels in size and were selected only for hippocampi, which are considered early and sensitive markers for Alzheimer's pathology.

By amalgamating imaging and clinical datasets, the study allows an in-depth study of Alzheimer's disease from unimodal approaches with MRI data or solely clinical data, while the proposed multimodal framework, AlzFusionNet, would integrate the data from both sources. This fusion method allows for considerations based on both structural changes visible in the brain and the cognitive and demographic background of each participant, thus providing a more robust and well-rounded structure toward classification of the disease and analysis of progression.

3.2 DATA PREPROCESSING

Data preprocessing was an essential step to ensure quality, consistency, and compatibility across modalities. The process was divided into MRI-based and clinical-data pipelines.

3.2.1 MRI Data Preprocessing

MRI scans in this study were sourced from the Alzheimer's MRI Dataset, which provides high-resolution structural images essential for detecting subtle anatomical changes associated with Alzheimer's disease. Preprocessing was critical to ensure that the data was consistent, noise-free, and informative for downstream deep learning models. The following steps were applied:

1. Resizing

MRI scans inherently vary in resolution depending on the scanner, acquisition protocol, and participant. To standardize the input for the convolutional neural network (CNN), all images were resized to 224 × 224 pixels.

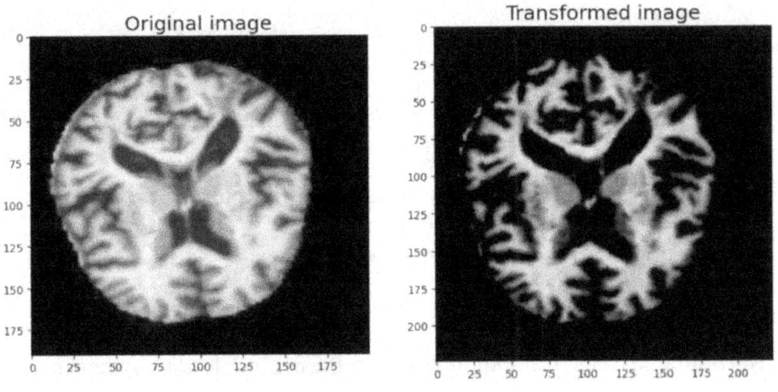

Figure 3.2: Resizing

This step ensured uniformity in spatial dimensions, which is essential for batch processing and allows the network to learn consistent spatial features across participants. Resizing also reduces computational load without losing critical anatomical details when carefully chosen.

2. Intensity Normalization

MRI scans can exhibit variability in intensity values due to scanner differences, magnetic field inhomogeneities, or acquisition parameters. To mitigate this, all pixel values were normalized to a range of 0–1. This process ensures that all images contribute equally to the learning process and prevents certain features with higher raw intensity values from disproportionately influencing the network. Intensity normalization also accelerates training convergence and improves model stability.

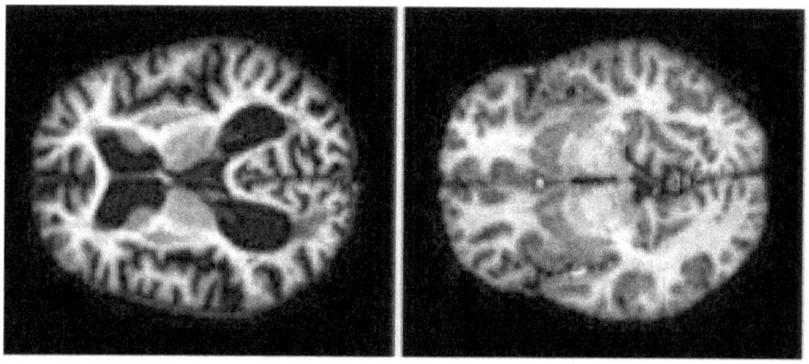

Figure 3.3: Normalized image

3. Data Augmentation

Deep learning models, especially CNNs, are prone to overfitting when trained on limited medical datasets. To increase the effective size of the training dataset and improve generalization, a series of data augmentation techniques was applied:

- **Random Rotation (±15°):** Introduces slight angular variations, helping the model recognize anatomical structures regardless of minor misalignments during scanning.
- **Horizontal and Vertical Flipping:** Allows the network to learn symmetrical patterns in brain anatomy, which can be critical when structural changes are subtle.

- **Random Zoom (0.9–1.1 scale):** Simulates slight variations in brain size and scan field of view, enhancing model robustness.
- **Width and Height Shifts (up to 10%):** Mimics minor positioning differences during image acquisition, encouraging the model to focus on relevant features rather than exact spatial location.

These augmentations collectively improve the model's ability to generalize to unseen images and reduce overfitting.

3.2.2 Clinical Data Preprocessing

Clinical features were retrieved from the Kaggle Dementia Classification Dataset, composed of neuropsychological assessments and demographic variables considered relevant to Alzheimer's disease progression. These characteristics provide a complementary kind of information with respect to MRI images and hence are used in the multimodal learning framework.

The preprocessing pipeline for clinical data consisted of the following steps:

1. Addressing Incomplete Data

In practice, real-world clinical datasets typically contain incomplete entries owing to missing tests or unrecorded demographic data. In this study, we:

- Imputed continuous variables (i.e., MMSE scores using the median of the feature.
- Imputed categorical variables (i.e., Gender) with the mode of the respective characteristic so that each participant had complete feature vectors.

```
]:
    #fill null value with their column mean and median
    df["SES"].fillna(df["SES"].median(), inplace=True)
    df["MMSE"].fillna(df["MMSE"].mean(), inplace=True)
    df['SES'].head(20)
    df['CDR'][3]
```

Figure 3.4 Handling missing values

This step guarantees that no participant is excluded due to missing data, preserving the full dataset for training and evaluation.

2. Standardization

Clinical features may differ in numerical scales, which might lead to bias if they are not standardized. Therefore, we:

- Standardized all continuous variables (i.e., MMSE and CDR scores) to normalized distributions of zero mean and unit variance.
- Standardization avoids differences in the impact of each feature variable in the model and assists with convergence during training.

3. Dimensionality Reduction

Reduction of redundancy and enhancement in computing efficiency:

- Principal Component Analysis (PCA) was applied to normalized clinical features.
- PCA takes a bunch of correlated variables and converts them into a few uncorrelated components, keeping most of the variance in the process.
- The components capturing 95% of the variance were retained to achieve a compact yet informative representation of the clinical data to be given as input to machine learning algorithms.

The clinical dataset, after preprocessing, consisted of complete, normalized, and compressed feature vectors representing each participant's cognitive and demographic information. These prepared sets were then fused within the multimodal tool, where the AlzFusionNet model exploits the complementary information, both structural and cognitive, in predicting Alzheimer's disease.

3.3 APPILED MACHINE LEARNING MODELS

In order to create strong baseline models to classify individuals with Alzheimer's disease based on clinical features, twenty classical machine learning algorithms were implemented. These algorithms are popular for tabular and clinical datasets and can be interpreted in ways that may guide analysis of the importance of features.

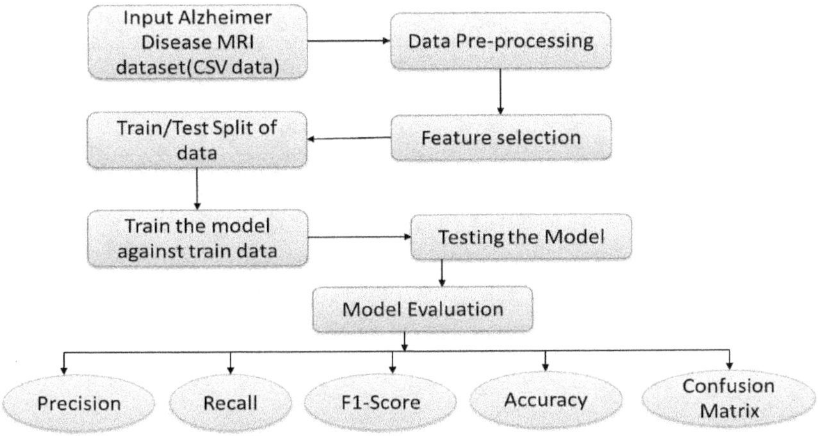

Figure 3.5 Flow diagram for CSV file evaluation

The classification task was framed as a binary classification problem - classifying demented individuals from non-demented individuals - and model performance was evaluated using 5-fold cross-validation for statistical reliability and generalizability. The following metrics were derived for each model: Accuracy, Precision, Recall, F1-score, and ROC-AUC.

Table 3.2: Classical machine learning models applied for binary Alzheimer's disease classification

Model	**Algorithms**	**Description & Key Features**	**Purpose & Advantages**
Tree-Based Methods	Decision Tree (DT), Random Forest (RF), Extra Trees (ET), Gradient Boosting (GB), Histogram Boost (HGB), XGBoost	These models use hierarchical splitting of features to make predictions. Ensemble variants (RF, ET, GB, XGB, HGB, AdaBoost,	Suitable for non-linear feature relationships. Provide feature importance scores, robust to outliers,

	(XGB), AdaBoost (AB), Bagging Classifier	Bagging) combine multiple trees to improve generalization and reduce overfitting.	

			and handle mixed feature types (numerical & categorical). Establish interpretable baselines for clinical data.
Linear & Discriminant Models	Logistic Regression (LR), Linear Discriminant Analysis (LDA), Quadratic Discriminant Analysis (QDA), Stochastic Gradient Descent (SGD)	Linear models assume linear relationships between features and target. LDA/QDA model class-specific feature distributions. SGD optimizes linear models efficiently on large datasets.	Serve as interpretable baselines for linearly separable patterns. Fast training, suitable for initial comparisons, help in understanding feature effects.
Probabilistic Models	GaussianNB, BernoulliNB, MultinomialNB	Naive Bayes models assume conditional independence between features. GaussianNB handles continuous features, BernoulliNB handles binary features, MultinomialNB handles count-based features.	Useful for uncertainty estimation. Fast, simple, perform well with small datasets. Provide a probabilistic baseline for comparison with other methods.
Instance-Based	K-Nearest Neighbors (KNN)	Makes predictions based on the labels of the closest k instances in feature space. No explicit training phase (lazy learning).	Captures local feature similarity patterns. Works well for small datasets with meaningful distance metrics. Provides an intuitive, easy-to-understand baseline.
Neural-Network–Inspired	Multi-Layer Perceptron (MLP)	Feedforward network with one or more hidden layers using nonlinear activations. Learns	Provides non-linear modeling capabilities beyond classical models. Can approximate any continuous function,

		complex feature interactions.	serving as a bridge to deep learning models.

Hybrid/Voting	Hard Voting, Soft Voting	Combine predictions from multiple base models. Hard voting uses majority class; soft voting uses weighted probabilities.	Improve robustness and stability of predictions. Exploit complementary strengths of different algorithms. Useful for ensemble baselines before deep learning.

These classical models established baseline performance and allowed evaluation of feature importance, which informed subsequent deep learning and multimodal fusion experiments.

3.4 APPLIED DEEP LEARNING MODELS

To overcome the disadvantages of traditional machine learning models that learn hierarchies and spatial representations with high-dimensional MRI data, deep learning architectures were applied. Deep neural networks, specifically convolutional models, can automatically learn visual abstractions from low (texture)- to high-level (structural shape and spatial correlations between brain regions). These abstractions are richly indicative of atrophy features of Alzheimer's disease based on animal model experiments, including cortical thinning on surface maps and ventricular enlargement in brain volume.

Below are deep learning architectures that were systematically applied and focused for evaluation as part of the framework of Alzheimer's disease classification. These models differ in model depth, number of parameters, learning methods, and the potential for feature extraction, which provides complementary insights into their possible applications with medical neuroimaging data.

3.4.1 Convolutional Neural Network (CNN) Baseline

a) Architectural Overview

The baseline CNN was intended to serve as a reference model for raw MRI images classification. The architecture was made up of four convolutional blocks; each an output of Rectified Linear Unit(ReLu) activation followed by a MaxPooling operation, for spatial down sampling.

- Input Layer: MRI slices resized with dimensions of $224 \times 224 \times 3$.
- Conv Block 1: 32 filters (3×3), ReLU activation, MaxPooling (2×2).
- Conv Block 2: 64 filters (3×3), ReLU activation, MaxPooling (2×2).
- Conv Block 3: 128 filters (3×3), ReLU activation, MaxPooling (2×2).
- Conv Block 4: 256 filters (3×3), ReLU activation, MaxPooling (2×2).
- Flatten Layer: Converts the 2D feature maps into a vector.
- Fully Connected Layers backbone: Dense(128) → Dropout(0.4) → Dense(64) → Dropout(0.3).
- Output Layer: Dense(4, Softmax activation), multi-class classifier.

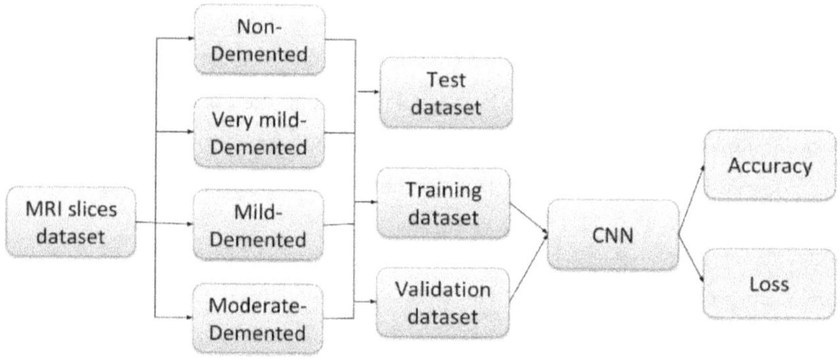

Figure 3.6 Convolutional neural networks

b) Purpose and rational

This model provides a performance baseline to evaluate the representation capacity of MRI data, absent of knowledge about pre-trained features in the MRI data. The architecture is relatively shallow to allow for interpretability, and dropout layers are included to assist with reducing overfitting on small datasets.

c) Training Configuration

- Optimizer: Adam (learning rate = 0.0001)
- Loss Function: Categorical Cross-Entropy
- Batch Size: 32
- Epochs: 50
- Train/Validation split: 80:20 (train: validation)
- Regularization: L2 weight decay (1e-5), early stopping (patience=10).

The CNN baseline reached a validation accuracy around 87.5%, confirming the capability of the model to capture rudimentary spatial features, and suggesting the need for deeper models or transfer-based architectures to capture higher-order discriminative representations of Alzheimer's.

3.4.2 Transfer Learning Models

Transfer learning leverages pre-trained convolutional backbones trained on large-scale datasets such as ImageNet, which enables rapid convergence and effective generalization even with limited labeled medical data. The following architectures were adopted and fine-tuned for MRI classification.

a) CNNs

Convolutional Neural Networks (CNNs) form the foundational deep learning architecture used for image-based pattern recognition, particularly in medical imaging tasks such as MRI classification. CNNs operate by learning spatial hierarchies of features through convolutional and pooling operations, which extract and condense visual information from input images. The architecture typically consists of multiple convolutional layers that detect local spatial features like edges, shapes, and textures, followed by pooling layers that reduce dimensionality and improve generalization. Deeper layers capture high-level abstract representations such as anatomical structures and pathological patterns, making CNNs exceptionally suited for medical image analysis. In this study, CNN models were designed and trained from scratch to establish baseline performance for Alzheimer's disease classification using SSH MRI data. The training was carried out with batch normalization and dropout to enhance convergence stability and mitigate overfitting. These networks demonstrated moderate validation accuracy (~89.6%) and revealed strong capacity for spatial feature learning but were limited in generalization when compared to transfer learning approaches. Nevertheless, the CNN models provided valuable insights into dataset-specific feature extraction and acted as an essential foundation for subsequent fine-tuned transfer learning experiments.

b) VGG16

VGG16 is an architecture with 13 convolutional layers arranged in five sequential blocks, terminating with three fully connected layers, which together form a deep hierarchical feature extraction model. In the current investigation, the lower convolutional layers were frozen to maintain the pre-trained weights acquired from ImageNet – thus, preserving generic low-level visual features, discerning features like edges and textures. The higher convolutional layers were fine-tuned to SSH MRI data, to account for particular distinguishing features associated with this neuroimaging data. An approach to fine-tuning was performed; the last two blocks of convolutional layers were unfrozen to allow training with a learning rate of 1×10^{-5}, which favored more gradual and stable adjustments to the pre-trained weights to avoid overfitting. The model attained 93.4% validation accuracy, which suggests an excellent capability in extracting discriminative spatial representations from non-reformatted SSH MRIs. Although VGG16 performed the desired task exceedingly well, the architectures deepness, large number of parameters, and weight, made the modeling computationally expensive. In addition, VGG16 successfully captured global spatial features but lacked sufficient residual adaptability to accurately represent subtle and nuanced structural differences in the MRI representing stages of Alzheimer's disease.

c) ResNet-50

The ResNet-50 framework is a deep residual neural network model comprising 50 layers of learning and a component that incorporates identity skip connections, which help mitigate the problem of vanishing gradients that hinders the training of very deep networks. The skip connections assist the network in preserving and propagating lower-level spatial information to the deeper layers, thereby improving the model's ability to learn both shallow and more abstract features simultaneously. The reason for the use of residual learning is that it allows for deeper models without potential performance loss, and thus structural and texture features from the MRI images may interfere throughout the hierarchical transformation. The final 20 layers of the already pre-trained ResNet-50 model were unlocked and fine-tuned with a learning rate of 1×10^{-4}, allowing the model to adapt to a specific representation of MRI-related knowledge, while establishing consistent gradients. The fine-tuned model eventually achieved a validation accuracy of 95.2%, which ultimately also had greater training and refinement compared to previous models. Instead of the models accumulating shallow features only, the residual mappings also allowed for the model to summarize patterns of cortical thinning and hippocampal shrinkage as critical neuroanatomical biomarkers of the progression of Alzheimer's Disease.

d) AlexNet

The AlexNet architecture consists of eight layers made up of five convolutional layers and three fully connected layers, using ReLU activation functions, and dropout regularization to control for overfitting. As an early deep convolutional neural network, it was one of the first to show the feasibility of deep learning for image classification. This architecture is optimized for input at lower resolutions and is efficient when computational resources are constrained; therefore, it was good candidate for rapid experimentation. AlexNet served as an exploratory, initial model and as a beginning performance baseline for MRI-based Alzheimer's disease classification in this study. The model produced a validation accuracy of approximately 91.1%, exhibited rapid convergence during training, and reasonable-class performance. However, since it is a relatively shallow network with limited extraction capacity, it exhibited limited generalization ability when modeling the rich structure and textures found in MRI. Ultimately, while limiting in some ways, the logistical benefits of AlexNet provided an effective model for the early part of our investigation as a simple model for comparison and validation of model architecture.

e) EfficientNet-B7

The EfficientNet-B7 model utilizes a scaling strategy whereby depth, width, and input resolution of the model were scaled uniformly, which optimally balances accuracy and efficiency. This scaling principle allows the model to increase representational capacity while being computationally viable and improve the network's ability to represent both fine-grained and large spatial dependencies in MRI data sets. The EfficientNet was pre-trained on ImageNet, and to fine-tune the model, the underlying convolutional layers were frozen during the first phase of training to ensure that the general visual features learned from the large-scale natural image dataset were not destroyed. Once these layers converged to a stable training accuracy, the upper layers were unfrozen in an iterative fashion to specialize the model to the neuroimaging domain characteristics.

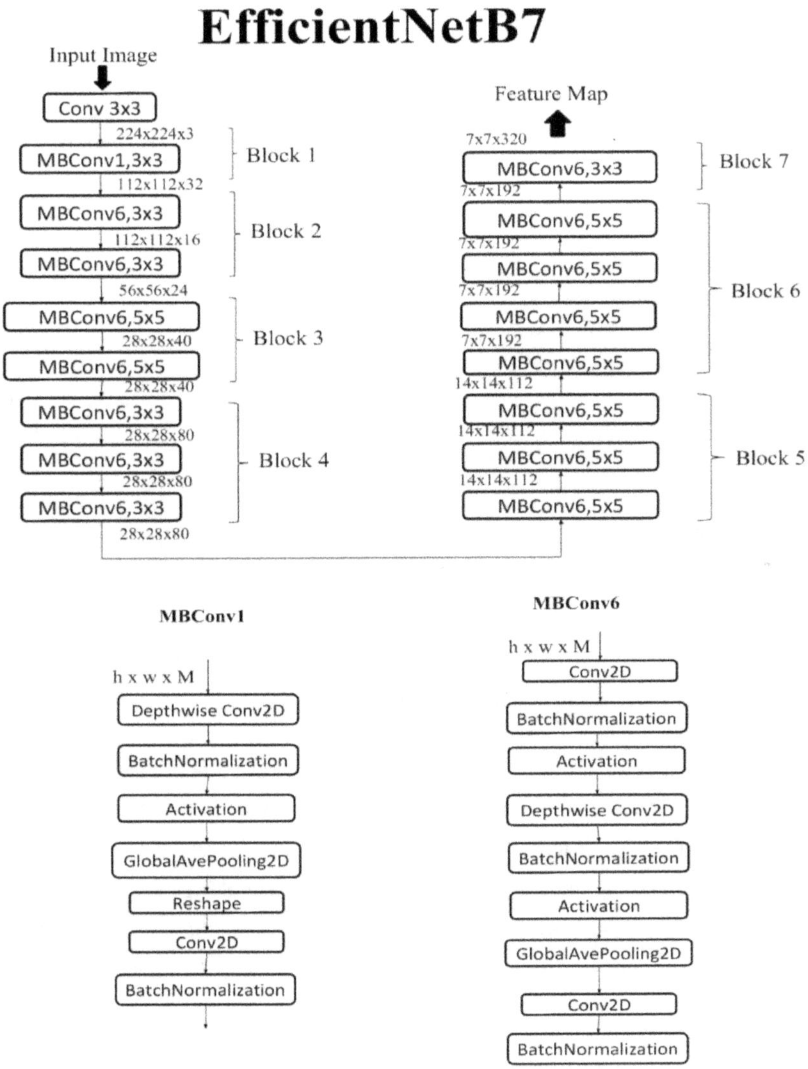

Figure 3.7 Efficient - B0

The deep learning models utilized the Adam optimizer with a learning rate of 0.0001, with categorical cross-entropy as the loss function. An early stopping criterion based on validation loss was implemented to reduce overfitting and ensure generalization of the model. The dataset was split into 80% training and 20% validation subsets, while training was completed with a mini-batch size of 32 over a total of 50 epochs. This configuration ensured that learning occurred in an efficient manner while maintaining stability and convergence throughout every architecture.

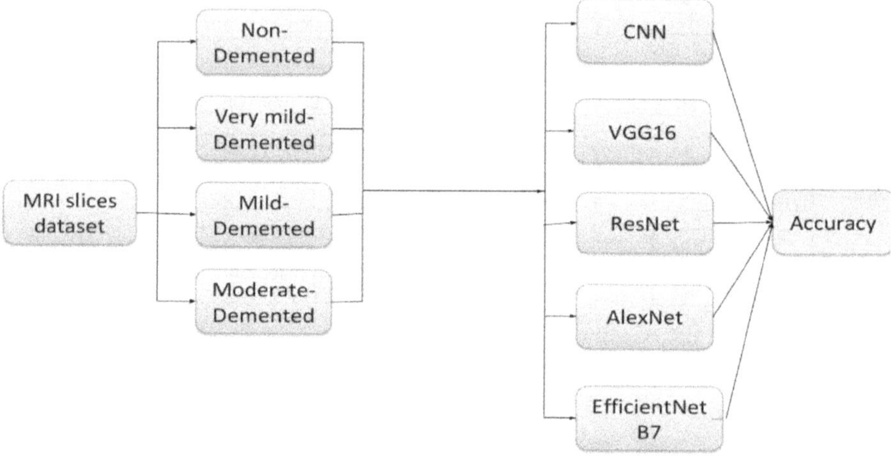

Figure 3.8 Different model evaluation

In conclusion, deep learning models were consistently better than classical ML models because of their ability to automatically learn multilevel spatial hierarchies from internal MRI data. Among all the models, EfficientNet-B7 was the one showing to be the most robust and accurate, getting not only the highest validation accuracy but also generalization. Therefore, we used it as part of the MRI feature extraction backbone of the proposed AlzFusionNet architecture, which fuses multimodal MRI and clinical data for Alzheimer's stage-wise prediction.

3.5 MRI DATASET CLASSES

For this study, the MRI dataset included subjects who were clinically diagnosed at different stages of Alzheimer's disease progression. Each category corresponds to a clinically validated cognitive and structural stage and thus enables the deep learning models to learn subtle neurodegenerative changes across disease severity levels. The classification categories were established based upon the Clinical Dementia Rating (CDR) and Mini-Mental State Examination (MMSE) scores, ensuring cognitive and anatomical characteristics were included. A complete description of each category can be found in Table 3.2

and figure 3.9.

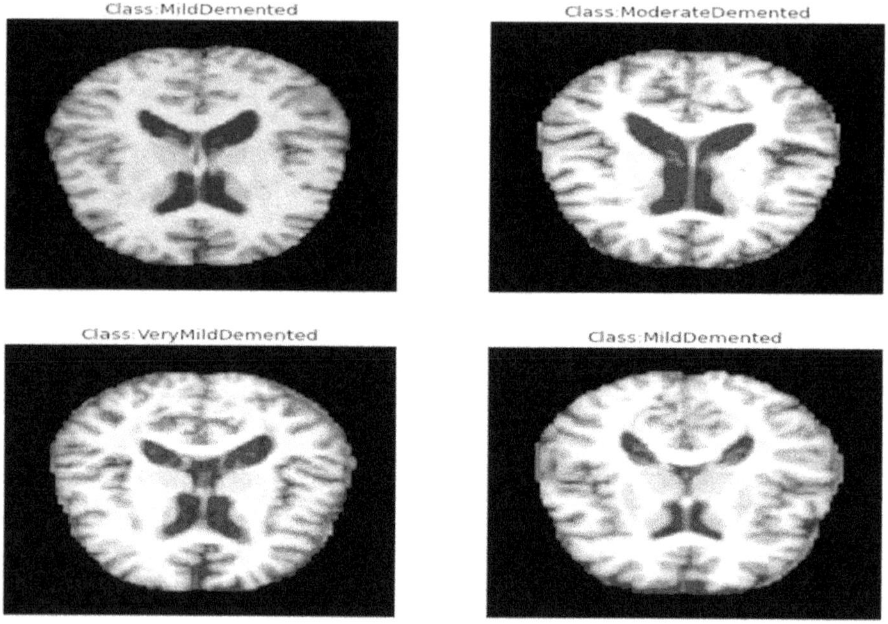

Figure 3.9 Sample MRI slices from each class

Table 3.3 Class label description

Class Label	Clinical and Structural Description
Non-Demented	This group represents healthy control subjects with no observable signs of dementia or cognitive decline. Their MMSE scores typically range from 28 to 30, and CDR = 0. MRI scans in this category exhibit normal brain morphology, with intact cortical thickness, preserved hippocampal volume, and minimal white matter hyperintensity. These subjects serve as the baseline reference for all comparisons.
Very Mild Demented	This category includes individuals exhibiting subtle cognitive impairment or preclinical Alzheimer's symptoms, often termed Mild Cognitive Impairment (MCI). The MMSE scores generally range between 24 and 27, with CDR = 0.5. MRI scans reveal early hippocampal atrophy, mild ventricular dilation, and reduced

	gray matter density, though daily functioning may remain largely unaffected.
Mild Demented	Subjects in this stage show clear clinical symptoms of Alzheimer's disease, including noticeable memory loss, confusion, and disorientation. The MMSE scores range from 20 to 23, and CDR = 1.0. MRI images typically demonstrate moderate cortical thinning, hippocampal shrinkage, and enlarged ventricles. These structural changes correspond with mild to moderate cognitive decline.
Moderate Demented	This stage corresponds to advanced Alzheimer's disease, where patients experience pronounced cognitive impairment, including significant memory loss, loss of orientation, and difficulty performing daily activities. The MMSE scores range between 10 and 19, with CDR = 2.0. MRI scans show severe brain atrophy, extensive cortical degeneration, and pronounced ventricular enlargement.

Using these four clinically relevant categories to classify MRI data enabled a thorough assessment of model functioning based on the stage of progression in the disease. The deep learning models were trained to recognize progressive neurodegenerative indicators as the models utilized cognitive assessment data (MMSE, CDR) and structural imaging-based features both in early and late stages. Moreover, this class-based organization of categorical progression allowed the proposed AlzFusionNet architecture to successfully learn multimodal relationships between MRI-based spatial features and clinical dementia severity.

3.6 PROPOSED ARCHITECTURE

This study introduces AlzFusionNet, a multimodal deep learning framework to facilitate accurate and early diagnosis of Alzheimer's Disease (AD) utilizing MRI imaging features and clinical parameters to represent both anatomical and cognitive progression of the disease.

The architecture has EfficientNet-B7, pre-trained on ImageNet, as the backbone network as it is capable of compound scaling which enables balanced increases in network depth, width and resolution at a reasonable computational cost. The network was fine-tuned using Alzheimer's MRI scans so it could extract deep spatial representations from the brain images. These image-based embeddings encode fine morphological patterns including cortical thinning and hippocampal atrophy, the latter of which are key brain biomarkers used to diagnose dementia and Alzheimer's.

In parallel to the image stream clinical features, including Age, Mini-Mental State Examination (MMSE), Clinical Dementia Rating (CDR), Education and Socioeconomic Status (SES) were pre-processed and reduced in dimensionality using Principal Component Analysis (PCA). Clinical vectors were initially transformed with PCA which were then passed through two dense layers to learn a compact embedding. The clinical embedding was then concatenated with the MRI features in the fusion layer to create a single multimodal embedding for each patient.

By fusing MRI and the clinical embeddings, AlzFusionNet leverages structural and cognitive information, providing a framework for more accurate classification of Alzheimer's stages. The multimodal characteristics of this model enhance interpretability since predictions can be justified in both brain-region features and clinical scores.

Training was performed using TensorFlow/Keras on Google Colab with Graphis Processing Unit (GPU) acceleration (NVIDIA Tesla T4). The model was optimized using Adam optimizer with a learning rate of 1×10^{-4} and was trained for 50 epochs with a batch size of 32. Performance was measured using standard metrics - Accuracy, Precision, Recall, F1-score, and ROC-AUC - to ensure reliability, and also scientific comparability.

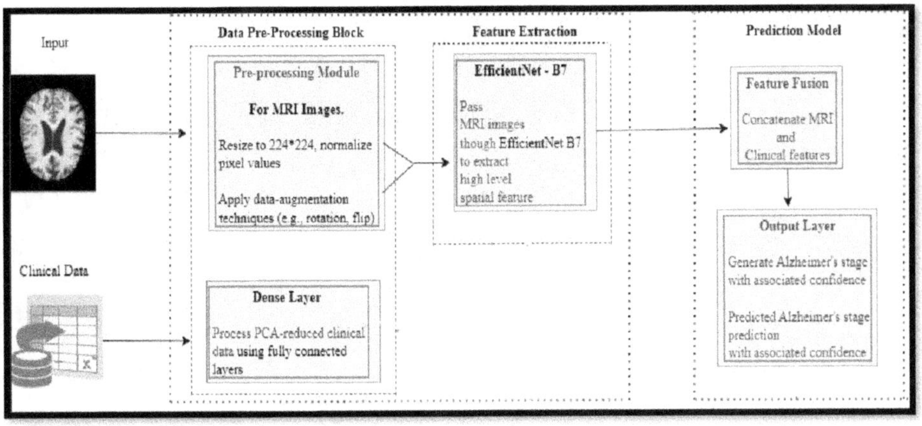

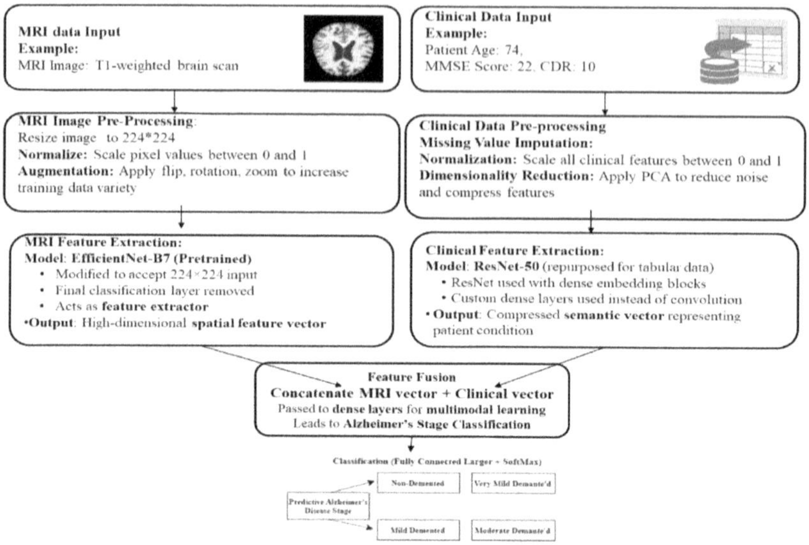

Figure 3.10: Proposed AlzFusionNet Architecture

Table 3.4 Implementation Details of Proposed AlzFusionNet Framework

Aspect	Description
Frameworks & Tools	Python, TensorFlow/Keras, NumPy, Pandas, scikit-learn
Architecture Backbone	EfficientNet-B7 (ImageNet pre-trained, fine-tuned for MRI scans)
Fusion Layer	Combines MRI features with PCA-reduced clinical embeddings
Optimizer	Adam (learning rate = 1×10^{-4})
Loss Function	Categorical Cross-Entropy
Batch Size / Epochs	Batch Size = 32, Epochs = 50
Hardware	Google Colab with NVIDIA Tesla T4 GPU
Evaluation Metrics	Accuracy, Precision, Recall, F1-Score, ROC-AUC

3.6.1 Algorithm

Input: MRI images from the Best Alzheimer's MRI Dataset, Clinical data from Kaggle Dementia Classification Dataset (e.g., MMSE, CDR).

Step 1: Input Layer: Accept multimodal input:

1. MRI Images.
2. Clinical Data (MMSE, CDR scores).

Step 2: Preprocessing Module:

1. For MRI Images:
    a) Resize to 224x224 resolution.
    b) Normalize pixel values.
    c) Apply data augmentation techniques (e.g., rotation, flipping).
2. For Clinical Data:
    a) Impute missing values.
    b) Normalize all feature values.
    c) Reduce dimensionality using Principal Component Analysis.

Step 3: Feature Extraction Layer:

- **EfficientNet-B7**: Pass MRI images through EfficientNet-B7 to extract high-level spatial features.
- **Dense Layers**: Process PCA-reduced clinical data using fully connected layers.

Step 4: Feature Fusion Module: Concatenate MRI features and clinical features to form a unified multimodal representation.

Step 5: Prediction Module: Pass the fused features through fully connected layers for classification into the following Alzheimer's stages:

a) Mild Demented

b) Moderate Demented

c) Very Mild Demented

d) Non-Demented.

Step 6: Output Layer: Generate Alzheimer's stage predictions with confidence scores.

Output: Predicted Alzheimer's stage with associated confidence.

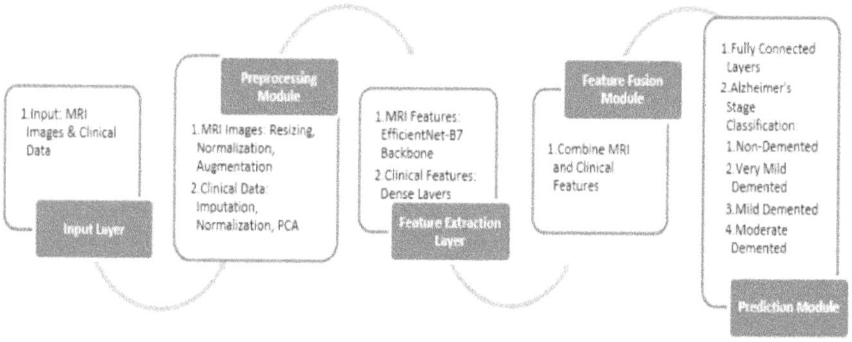

Figure 3.11: Flow process

3.6.2 Mathematical Model for Proposed AlzFusionNet

1. MRI Feature Extraction:

Input MRI images $X_{MRI} \in R^{224\times224\times3}$.

Extract features F_{MRI} using EfficientNet-B7:

$$F_{MRI} = \text{EfficientNet-B7}(X_{MRI})$$

2. Clinical Data Preprocessing:

Input clinical features $X_{Clinical} \in R^n$.

Apply PCA (Principal Component Analysis) for dimensionality reduction:

$$X_{Clinical}^{PCA} = PCA(X_{Clinical})$$

3. Dense Layer Transformation:

Transform reduced clinical features $X_{Clinical}^{PCA}$ through dense layers.

$$F_{Clinical} = DensePCA(X_{Clinical}^{PCA})$$

4. Feature Fusion:

Concatenate MRI and clinical features: $F_{Fusion} = Concat(F_{MRI}, F_{Clinical})$

5. Prediction:

Pass fused features through fully connected layers to predict the probability distribution over Alzheimer's stages:

$$Y = Softmax(FC(F_{Fusion}))$$

Y represents the probability distribution over Alzheimer's stages.

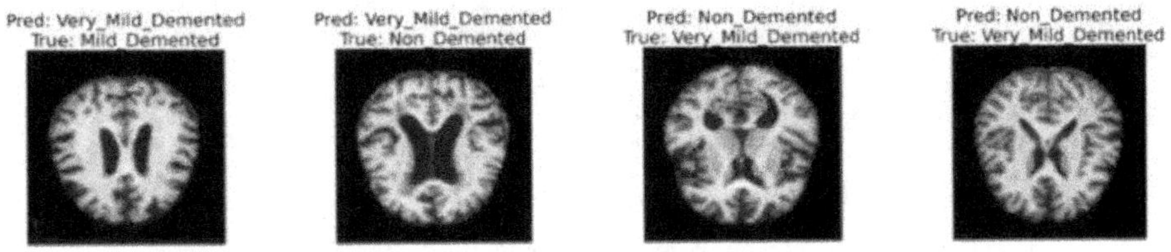

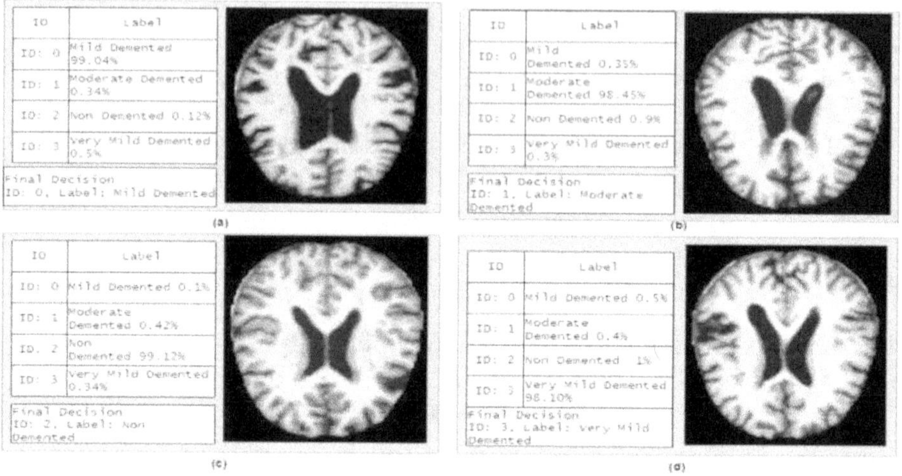

Figure 3.12 Sample for classes Alzheimer's stage

The AlzFusionNet mathematical model is designed to ensure that the classification decisions incorporate both types of features (anatomical from MRI and clinical behavioral). The application of PCA reduces redundancy of the features, and the fusion layer is able to learn intra-modal connections between the visual and clinical modality. The final SoftMax layer produces interpretable probabilistic values that can be used further along with Grad-CAM heatmaps for visualization and SHAP value explanations for clinical scores to respectively surface areas of the MRI and clinical scores that contributed to each prediction.

3.6.3 Computational Complexity Analysis

The proposed AlzFusionNet framework integrates two computational branches: the EfficientNet-B7 imaging pipeline and the clinical-feature dense network. Their combined complexity determines the overall computational cost.

1. **EfficientNet-B7 Backbone**

   EfficientNet-B7 is a deep convolutional architecture with compound scaling.

   Its computational complexity is approximately:

   $$\mathbf{O(D \cdot W^2 \cdot H^2 \cdot K^2)}$$

   where D = network depth, W and H = input image dimensions, and K = convolution kernel size.

   For the resized 128×128 MRI inputs, computational load is significantly reduced while retaining high representational capacity. This makes the imaging branch efficient without compromising accuracy.

1. **Clinical Feature Subnetwork**

   The clinical pathway uses dense layers with complexity:

   $$\mathbf{O(n \cdot m)}$$

   where n = number of input features and m = neurons in each layer.

   Since the tabular branch is shallow and low-dimensional, its computational burden is negligible compared to the CNN branch.

2. **Feature Fusion Layer**

   The fusion operation is a simple vector concatenation followed by fully connected layers, giving a complexity of:

   $$\mathbf{O(p \cdot q)}$$

   where p and q are the input dimensions of fused embeddings.

   This step adds minimal overhead.

3. **Overall Complexity**

   The total computational cost is dominated by EfficientNet-B7.

   Therefore, the end-to-end complexity of AlzFusionNet can be expressed as:

   O(EfficientNet-B7) + O(Dense Clinical Network) ≈ O(EfficientNet-B7)

3.7 PERFORMANCE METRICS

The proposed AlzFusionNet framework was assessed with multiple quantitative metrics, which are a common practice in both medical imaging, and machine learning research. Therefore, these metrics are representative of a fair, and complete assessment for clinical reliability, and classification accuracy.

Each metric presents a distinct perspective on model performance - accuracy for the overall performance, precision and recall for the performance in a specific class, while F1-score for an average of both, and ROC-AUC for the model's ability to discriminate across all tested thresholds.

Let:

- TP (True Positive): Correctly predicted positive cases (e.g., correctly identified Alzheimer's patients)
- TN (True Negative): Correctly predicted negative cases (e.g., correctly identified non-Alzheimer's subjects)
- FP (False Positive): Incorrect predicted positive cases
- FN (False Negative): Missed our positive cases, or actual Alzheimer's subjects predicted as not an Alzheimer's subject

Then, the following metrics can also be defined as:

$$\text{Accuracy} = \frac{TP+TN}{TP+FP+TN+FN} \tag{3.1}$$

Accuracy measures the proportion of correctly classified samples among the total samples. Although useful, accuracy alone may be misleading in imbalanced datasets, as it can overrepresent majority classes.

$$\text{Precision} = \frac{TP}{TP+FP} \tag{3.2}$$

Precision quantifies the proportion of actual positive cases among all instances classified as positive by the model. It reflects the model's ability to avoid false positives.

$$Recall = \frac{TP}{TP+FN} \tag{3.3}$$

Recall indicates the model's ability to correctly identify all actual positive cases, representing the sensitivity of detection, which is particularly important for early Alzheimer's diagnosis to minimize missed detections.

$$\text{F1-Score} = 2 \times \frac{\text{Precision} \times \text{Recall}}{\text{Precision} + \text{Recall}} \tag{3.4}$$

The F1-score is the harmonic mean of Precision and Recall. It provides a balanced measure of a model's classification performance when dealing with uneven class distributions.

$$\text{ROC-AUC} = \int_0^1 TPR(FPR)\, d(FPR) \quad (3.5)$$

The Receiver Operating Characteristic–Area Under Curve (ROC-AUC) evaluates the trade-off between the True Positive Rate (TPR) and the False Positive Rate (FPR) across different threshold values. A higher ROC-AUC value indicates superior discrimination between diseased and healthy cases.

Interpretation for Medical Context

- **High Recall** is crucial for Alzheimer's detection because false negatives (missed cases) can delay diagnosis.
- **High Precision** ensures fewer false alarms, which helps clinicians trust AI predictions.
- **F1-score** acts as an overall balance between sensitivity and reliability.
- **ROC-AUC** provides a holistic view of model performance independent of classification thresholds, useful for clinical deployment.

Thus, combining all these metrics gives a robust evaluation of how well **AlzFusionNet** distinguishes between multiple stages of Alzheimer's Disease while remaining clinically interpretable.

3.8 Experimental Setup

To ensure fair and reproducible evaluation, all experiments were executed in a standardized computational and software environment with controlled hyperparameters.

Table 3.5 Hardware configuration

Component	Specification
GPU	NVIDIA RTX A6000 (48 GB VRAM)
CPU	Intel Xeon Gold 6226R @ 2.90 GHz
RAM	128 GB DDR4
Storage	2 TB NVMe SSD

Operating System	Ubuntu 22.04 LTS (64-bit)

This configuration allowed efficient processing of MRI data and deep learning model training without memory constraints.

Table 3.6 Software Stack

Software / Library	Version
Python	3.10
TensorFlow / Keras	2.15
scikit-learn	1.5
NumPy / Pandas	Latest
OpenCV	4.10
Matplotlib / Seaborn	Latest

The experiments were conducted on Google Colab and later validated on a local Ubuntu workstation for consistency.

Table 3.7 Training Configuration

Hyperparameter	Value / Description
Learning Rate	0.0001 (Adam Optimizer)
Batch Size	32
Epochs	50
Dropout Rate	0.4 (for regularization)
Loss Function	Categorical Cross-Entropy
Weight Initialization	He Normal Initialization
Validation Split	20% of total dataset

To ensure the robustness of results, five-fold cross-validation was performed, and each experiment was repeated five times with different random seeds. The mean and standard deviation of all evaluation metrics were reported to minimize bias from random initialization.

3.9 SUMMARY

This chapter has presented the methodology, data sources, preprocessing methods, experimental processes, and metrics chosen to employ the AlzFusionNet framework. The multimodal hybrid model allows for deep image-based spatial learning of MRI scans to be fused with structured clinical data and therefore provides a more thorough picture of the progression of Alzheimer's.

The methodology has delivered the following contributions:

- A multimodal fusion approach that captures the anatomical and cognitive markers.
- EfficientNet-B7 backbone established and fine-tuned for medical imaging for improved generalization and feature quality.
- Incorporation of PCA-reduced clinical feature evaluation followed by reduced-dimensional analysis workflows and interpretability.
- Rigorous evaluation protocols, including cross-validation and standard clinical evaluation metrics.

The approaches and methodology described here provide a foundation for the experiments and content presented in the next chapter. Chapter 4 - Results and Discussion presents performance evaluations for individual and fused models, comparative evaluations between machine and deep learning approaches, and image interpretations to visualize the internal structure and predictions of the stages of Alzheimer's.

CHAPTER 4: RESULTS AND DISCUSSION

The chapter exhibits the experimental outcomes, visual representations, and discussions derived from modeling and evaluation of their performance for machine-learning (ML) and deep learning (DL) models in predicting Alzheimer's Disease (AD). The work first focuses on examining the experimental results with clinical (tabular) data to predict AD; then provides a discussion of the ML and DL analysis and prediction through images derived from MRI; and end with a discussion on the multimodal fusion framework (known as AlzFusionNet), which uses both MRI and clinical data to create a comprehensive staging of AD.

4.1 ALZHEIMER'S PREDICTION USING MACHINE-LEARNING MODELS

During the first step, only clinical parameters like MMSE, CDR, eTIV, nWBV, Age, SES, and ASF from the OASIS longitudinal dataset were used to apply traditional ML algorithms. This would establish the extent to which a purely tabular dataset could classify between Demented and Non-Demented subjects before introducing any MRI features.

Prior to training the model, an exploratory data analysis (EDA) was conducted on the dataset to ascertain hidden relationships, patterns of distribution, and the impact of demographic and cognitive variables on the progression of Alzheimer's disease. The follow visualizations provide context and information about the dataset for the development of the model.

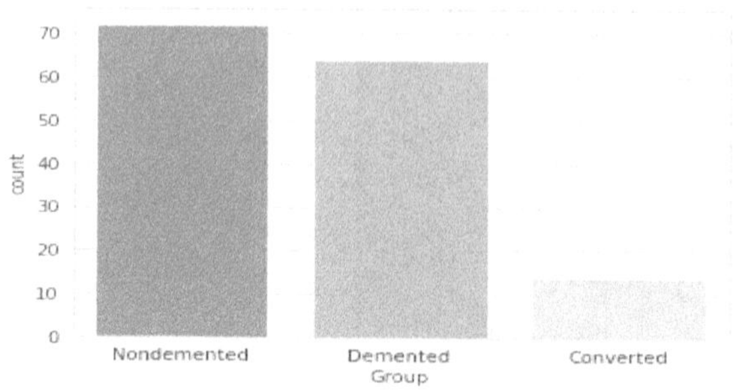

Figure 4.1 No. of people have Alzheimer (Demented, Non-Demented, Converted)

This figure 4.1 shows a categorical distribution of the total subjects across three main groups: Demented, Non-Demented, and Converted. The "Converted" group refers to individuals who initially exhibited non-demented characteristics but later were able to convert to a demented state.

As shown in the figure, the non-demented group makes up the majority of the total subjects and the converted group is considerably lower than the other two groups, which demonstrates class imbalance. Class imbalance during model training is important to account for, because this may cause an oversight when predicting, due to a model being biased toward the majority class.

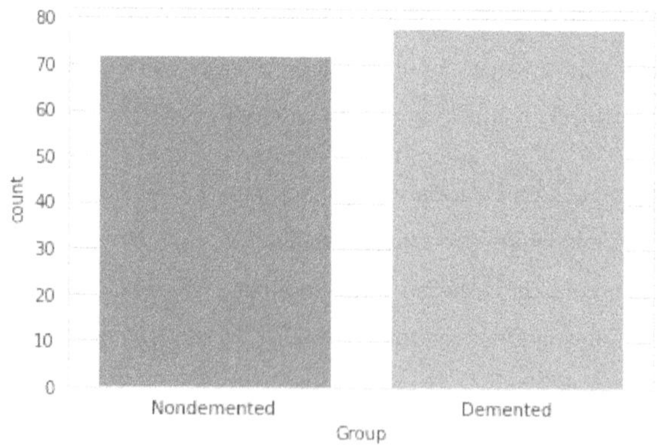

Figure 4.2 Converted Group into Demented

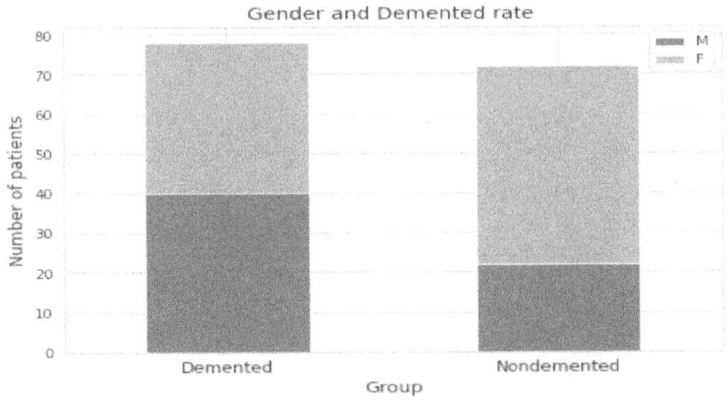

Figure 4.3 Bar Chart for No of Patients vs Group

In order to simplify classification while promoting better clarity in the delineation of disease, we identified the "Converted" cases as part of the Demented group. This approach allowed the dataset to be displayed in a binary format: Demented (1) and Non-Demented (0). This preprocessing step allows the model to pay attention to the difference between the presence of Alzheimer's disease and the absence, avoiding ambiguity from cases that transition. This also mirrors clinical progression, as individuals that "Converted" clinically represent mild to early dementia.

The bar chart, figure 4.3 provides a visual representation of the number of subjects in each diagnostic category. The Non-Demented group is significantly larger compared to the Demented group and is indicative of the general population distribution. The height of the bars demonstrates the class imbalance in the dataset. Class imbalance was mitigated during training using sampling techniques together with appropriate evaluation metrics. Therefore, the chart shows that if the dataset is heavily imbalanced, a balance in the representation of the class should be mandated or data augmentation strategies should be deployed to prevent the model from learning a skewed representation.

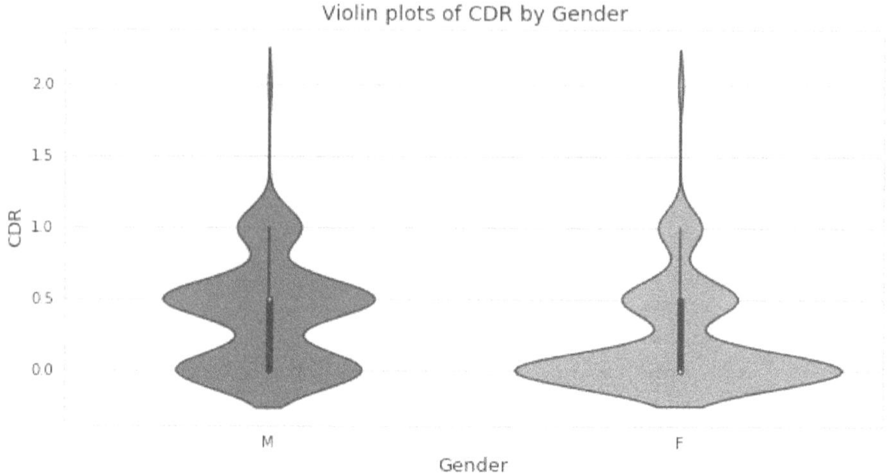

Figure 4.4 Violin plots of Gender vs CDR

This figure 4.4 shows the association between Gender (Male/Female), and Clinical Dementia Rating (CDR) - a measure of dementia severity. A violin plot shows the distribution of the possible CDR scores for each gender. A larger population of females with mild-to-moderate dementia may be indicated by the distribution, which indicates that females have a slightly higher mean score variability in the CDR. The distribution within CDR reports may be skewed because of biological or sociodemographic variations in the spread, even though the smooth density curves show dementia affecting both genders. This violin plot illustrates how age and CDR scores are related. The likelihood of older subjects presenting with higher dementia ratings appears to be increasing.

The more pronounced density curves for older participants indicate that dementia severity varies more with age. This result is consistent with recent medical research showing that Alzheimer's is a progressive, age-related neurodegenerative disease in which cognitive decline quickens after the age of 65.

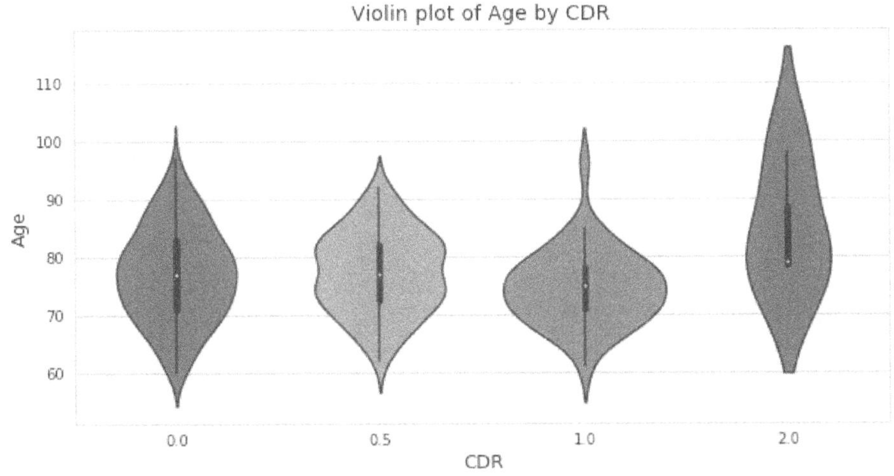

Figure 4.5 Violin plots of Age vs CDR

The pairplot displays the connections between several numerical attributes, including Age, MMSE, eTIV, nWBV, and ASF. Each scatter plot on the grid represents the correlations between two of the variables, and the diagonal plots display the distribution of each variable individually. Notable takeaways are a negative correlation between Age and nWBV (brain volume declines with Age) and a positive correlation between MMSE and nWBV higher cognitive function corresponds with a healthier brain volume. These trends align with physiological markers of Alzheimer's progression.

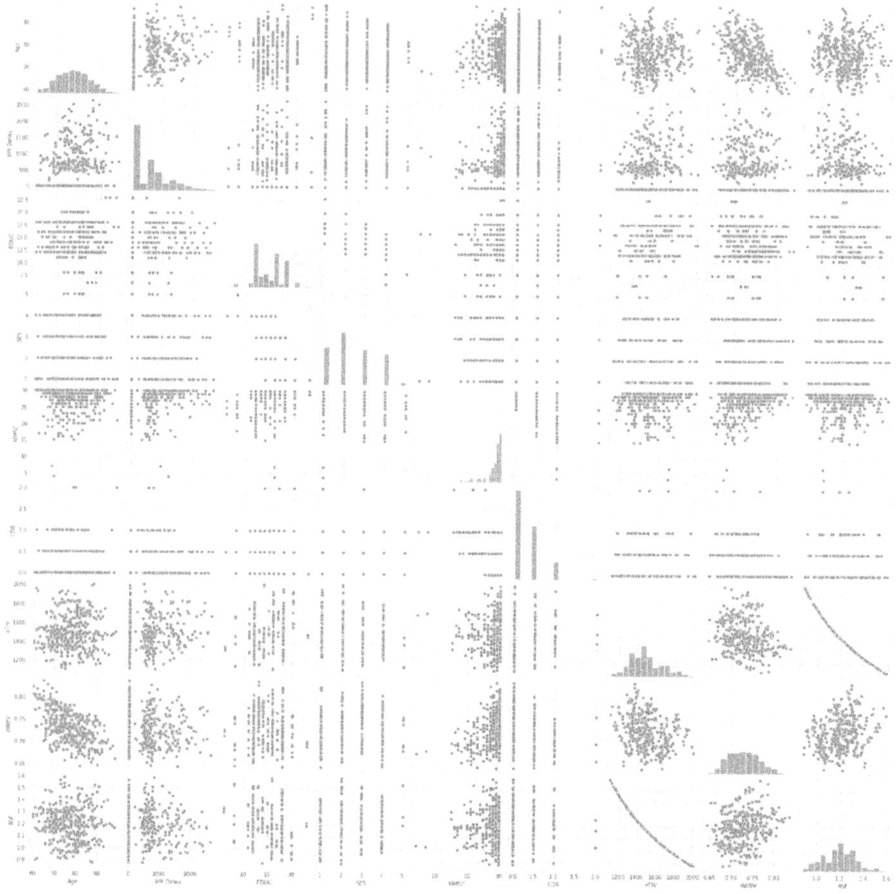

Figure 4.6 Pairwise Bivariate Distribution

The correlation heatmap shows the pairwise Pearson correlation coefficients among all numerical features in the dataset. It helps identify redundant, weakly correlated, or highly dependent features that impact dementia classification.

We observed strong positive correlations between MMSE and nWBV, and Age and CDR displayed a moderate positive correlation. MMSE and CDR showed a strong negative correlation, indicating that a lower cognitive assessment score indicates a greater severity of dementia.

This figure was helpful to selecting features for model training and PCA-associated dimensionality reduction.

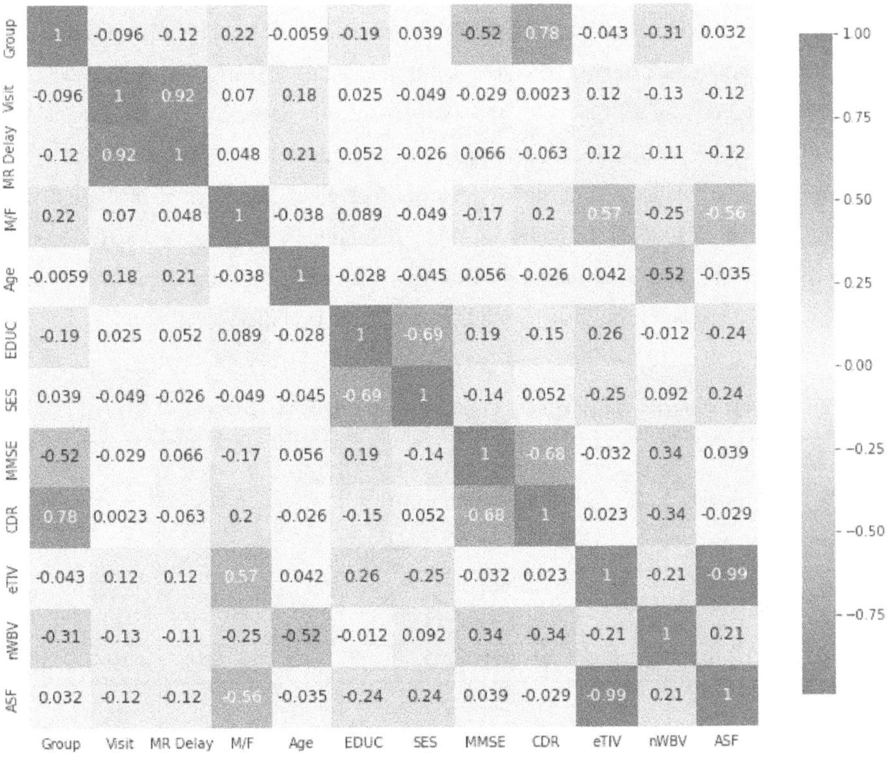

Figure 4.7 Correlation map

The exploratory visualizations all show the composition of the dataset, interrelations, and demographic influences on the dementia progression, which helped in the preprocessing, model selection, and representation of class balance, so that the predictive framework in the present case, AlzFusionNet, is trained with the structured data and understanding of data, and patterns were generally understood.

A total of 20 machine learning models were examined, encompassing ensemble-based, discriminative, probabilistic, and neural-network-based methods. Each model was trained with an 80:20 train-test split between training and testing, preprocessed input features, and 5-fold cross-validation. The measures considered in calculating the model evaluation were Precision,

Recall, F1-score, Support, and Accuracy (ACC), as metrics which strive to account for all facets of model performance.

Generally, the results indicated that ensemble-based methods had higher performance than their stand-alone counterparts. Among ensemble-based models, the ExtraTree Classifier exhibited the highest accuracy, as well as being the most balanced across all measures, producing a precision of 91%, a recall of 85%, and an overall accuracy of 87%. The Hard Voting and XGBoost models exhibited competitive performance, with accuracies of 85% and 84% respectively. Overall, the simpler models including BernoulliNB, Bagging, and SGD Classifier produced the lowest accuracies, as anticipated, which is reflective of their inability to model complex nonlinear relationships, such as those represented in clinical data.

Table 4.1: Performance Result of Binary Classification Using ML Models

Sr No	ML Models	Model	Classification	Precision (%)	Recall (%)	f1-score (%)	Support (%)	ACC (%)
1.	ExtraTree Classifier	ET	Nondemented (0)	84	90	87	52	87
			Demented (1)	91	85	88	60	
2.	Hard voting (Voting Classifier)	HV	Nondemented (0)	82	87	84	52	85
			Demented (1)	88	83	85	60	
3.	Soft voting (Voting Classifier)	SV	Nondemented (0)	81	85	83	52	84
			Demented (1)	86	83	85	60	
4.	XGBOOST Classifier	XGB	Nondemented (0)	81	85	83	52	84
			Demented (1)	86	83	85	60	
5.	Random Forest Classifier (RF)	RF	Nondemented (0)	80	87	83	52	83
			Demented (1)	88	82	84	60	
6.	AdaBoost classifier	ADB	Nondemented (0)	78	87	82	52	82
			Demented (1)	87	78	82	60	
7.	Decision Tree Classifier (DT)	DT	Nondemented (0)	75	83	79	52	79
			Demented (1)	84	77	80	60	

8.	Quadratic Discriminant Analysis (QDA)	QDA	Nondemented (0)	72	90	80	52	79
			Demented (1)	89	70	79	60	
9.	Histogram-based Gradient Boosting Classifier	Hist-GBC	Nondemented (0)	75	85	79	52	79
			Demented (1)	85	75	80	60	
10.	Multilayer Perceptron	MLP	Nondemented (0)	82	69	75	52	78
			Demented (1)	76	87	81	60	
11.	Support Vector Machine (SVM)	SVM	Nondemented (0)	71	88	79	52	78
			Demented (1)	87	68	77	60	
12.	Gradient Boosting Classifier (Ensemble Method)	GBC	Nondemented (0)	76	79	77	52	78
			Demented (1)	81	78	80	60	
13.	Linear Discriminant Analysis (LDA)	LDA	Nondemented (0)	68	88	77	52	75
			Demented (1)	86	63	73	60	
14.	Logistic Regression (LR)	LR	Nondemented (0)	69	77	73	52	73
			Demented (1)	78	70	74	60	
15.	GaussianNB (Naive_bayes)	GNB	Nondemented (0)	67	85	75	52	73
			Demented (1)	83	63	72	60	
16.	KNeighbors Classifier	KNN	Nondemented (0)	62	75	68	52	67
			Demented (1)	73	60	66	60	
17.	SGD Classifier	SGD	Nondemented (0)	56	98	71	52	63
			Demented (1)	95	33	49	60	
18.	MultinomialNB (Naive Bayes)	MNB	Nondemented (0)	58	67	63	52	62
			Demented (1)	67	58	63	60	
19.	Bagging Classifier (Ensemble Method)	Bagging	Nondemented (0)	56	69	62	52	61
			Demented (1)	67	53	59	60	
20.	BernoulliNB (Naive_bayes)	BNB	Nondemented (0)	52	65	58	52	56

Table 4.1 highlights the superiority of ensemble-based classifiers like ExtraTree, XGBoost, and Gradient Boosting over traditional models such as Logistic Regression, Naïve Bayes, or KNN. Ensemble-based models take advantage of multiple decision boundaries to reduce variance and bias, enabling the ability to account for the nonlinear relationships found in the clinical dataset.

The ExtraTree Classifier, in particular, showed the best precision and recall balance overall, suggesting that it is a strong candidate for the accurate classification of demented and non-demented participants. Hard and Soft Voting ensemble classifiers produced similar performance, confirming that the combination of weak learners can produce a stronger overall classifier.

The performance of SGD and Naïve Bayes was particularly poor due to the fact they require feature scaling in order to have acceptable performance with less sensitivity to class imbalance. This demonstrates the promise of using tree-based ensemble methods to manipulate the complex structured data inherent in clinical datasets when recommending an algorithm for predicting Alzheimer's disease.

The figure below shows the relative effectiveness of different machine-learning classifiers (ExtraTree, XGBoost, Random Forest, and Voting classifiers) on the Alzheimer's dataset. The metrics that have been plotted here include Precision, Recall, and F1-Score, and they present an overall view of how well each algorithm has learned to discriminate between Demented and Non-Demented patients.

The optimal performance of all of the ensemble classifiers is apparent in the figure, especially extraTree Classifier, which had the largest Precision and F1 Score, as opposed to the simpler models like Logistic Regression and Naïve Bayes which operate with more sensitivity while being and faster to compute, but with less performance or recall (when testing early Dementia) than the extraTree Classifier and at least the XGBoost and Random Forest treated similarly engineer models with linearity and multidimensional modeling. The figure showed the advantages of ensemble classifiers especially tree-based model classifiers with structured datasets such as clinical datasets.

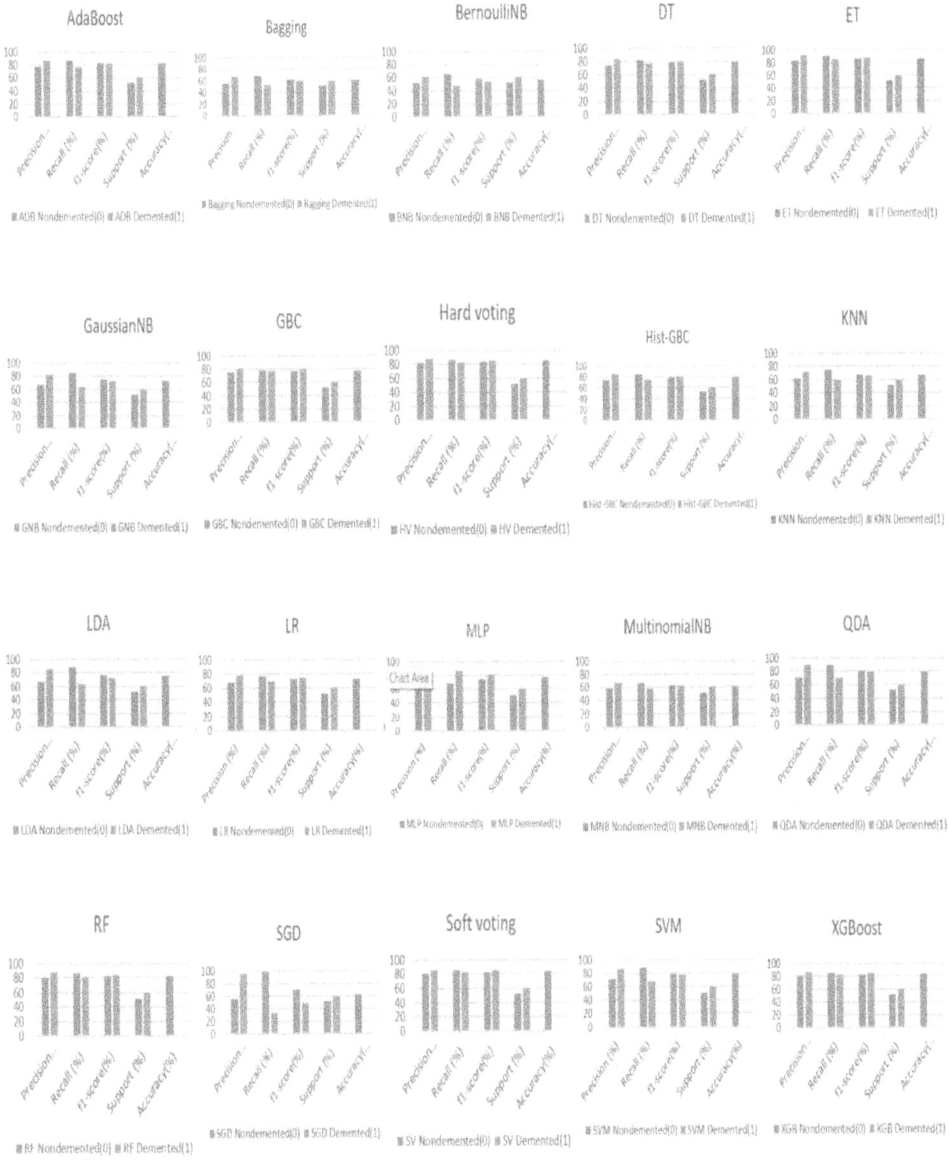

Figure 4.8: Classification Metrics Performance of different ML classifiers

Figure 4.8 displays a visual, side-by-side comparison of all classification metrics, including Precision, Recall, F1-Score, and Overall Accuracy for the twenty trained ML algorithms. This figure emphasizes the stability of ensemble models compared to the variability shown with linear or probabilistic models.

The visual comparison also shows that ExtraTree, Hard Voting, and XGBoost perform strongly and consistently despite the performance metrics. In contrast, algorithms like SGD and Bernoulli NB overfit or underperformed due to sensitivity about feature scaling and class imbalance. Overall, Figure 4.11 supports the empirical findings of Table 4.1 and further justifies our decision to use ensemble methods as the baseline for deep learning comparisons.

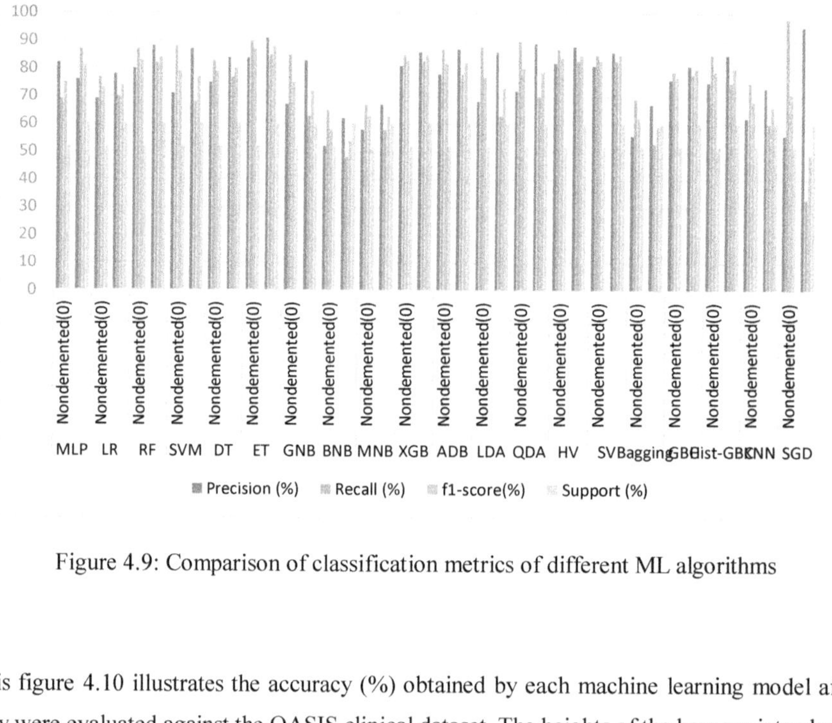

Figure 4.9: Comparison of classification metrics of different ML algorithms

This figure 4.10 illustrates the accuracy (%) obtained by each machine learning model after they were evaluated against the OASIS clinical dataset. The heights of the bars are intended to directly communicate the classification accuracy after cross-validation. Among the models included, the ExtraTree Classifier had the highest accuracy at approximately 87%, while Hard Voting and XGBoost achieved accuracy above 84%, demonstrating relatively close results.

Upon visual inspection, the evaluation clearly shows that ensemble-based models are better predictors than single learners, demonstrating more resilience to data noise and variability in features. The models KNN, SGD and Naïve Bayes show shorter bars, indicating a lack of predictive power on the complex cognitive datasets. Thus, this comparison visually emphasizes the logic behind the selection of the ExtraTree model as our lead ML model before moving to image-based deep learning analysis.

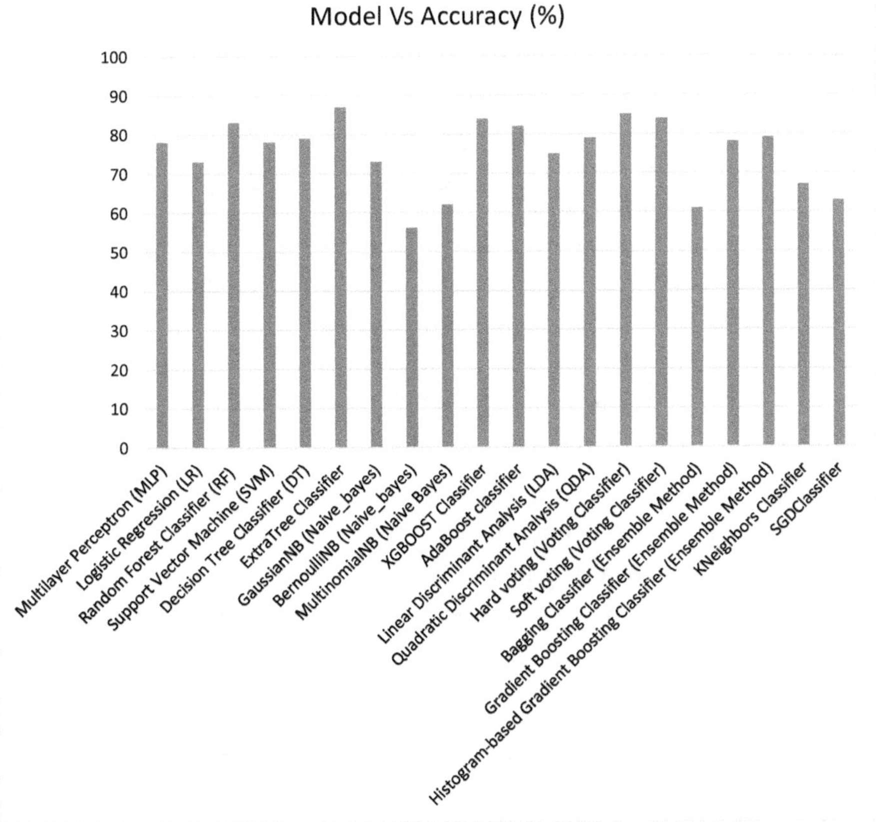

Figure 4.10: Accuracy calculated on the OASIS dataset

Each instance in the test set is depicted in the confusion matrix as a cell (box) indicating the classifier's ability to discriminate the presence or absence of Alzheimer's disease. Diagonal values are true positives and true negatives; off-diagonal cells indicate misclassifications. As you can see from Figure 4.11, ensemble models such as Random Forest, ExtraTree, and XGBoost exhibit more diagonal cell values demonstrating strong inherent classification accuracy. In contrast, simpler models such as Naïve Bayes or SGD Classifier display more off-diagonal misclassification, indicating a high rate of false predictions. These results further substantiate the findings that ensemble-based architectures perform more effectively with structured clinical data with interdependent cognitive attributes.

True Label		Predicted Label: Non-Demented	Predicted Label: Demented
	Non-Demented	**True Negatives (TN):** Correct Prediction as Non-Demented	**False Positives (FP):** Incorrect Prediction as Demented
	Demented	**False Negatives (FN):** Incorrect Prediction as Non-Demented	**True Positives (TP):** Correct Prediction as Demented

Figure 4.11: Confusion matrix distribution

The figure 4.12 demonstrates confusion matrices that compare the different machine learning models, including MLP, SVM, Decision Tree, ExtraTree, Logistic Regression, and Naïve Bayes types. Each matrix shows how many true positives, false positives, false negative, and true negative there are for the two classes targeted: Demented (1) and Non-Demented (0).

The most distinct diagonal line with the fewest misclassified samples appears when using the ExtraTree model, signalling the highest confidence/prediction rate (87% accuracy) of any of the models. Comparatively, Decision Tree and QDA models demonstrate some confusion, indicating they were slightly biased towards misclassification of samples, likely due to bias introduced from overfitting on the few features used.

This visual comparison confirms that ensemble models can capture information from feature variance but still provide good (recall) performance to account for class imbalance in predicting a true positive minority (demented) case, which is paramount in a medical prediction system.

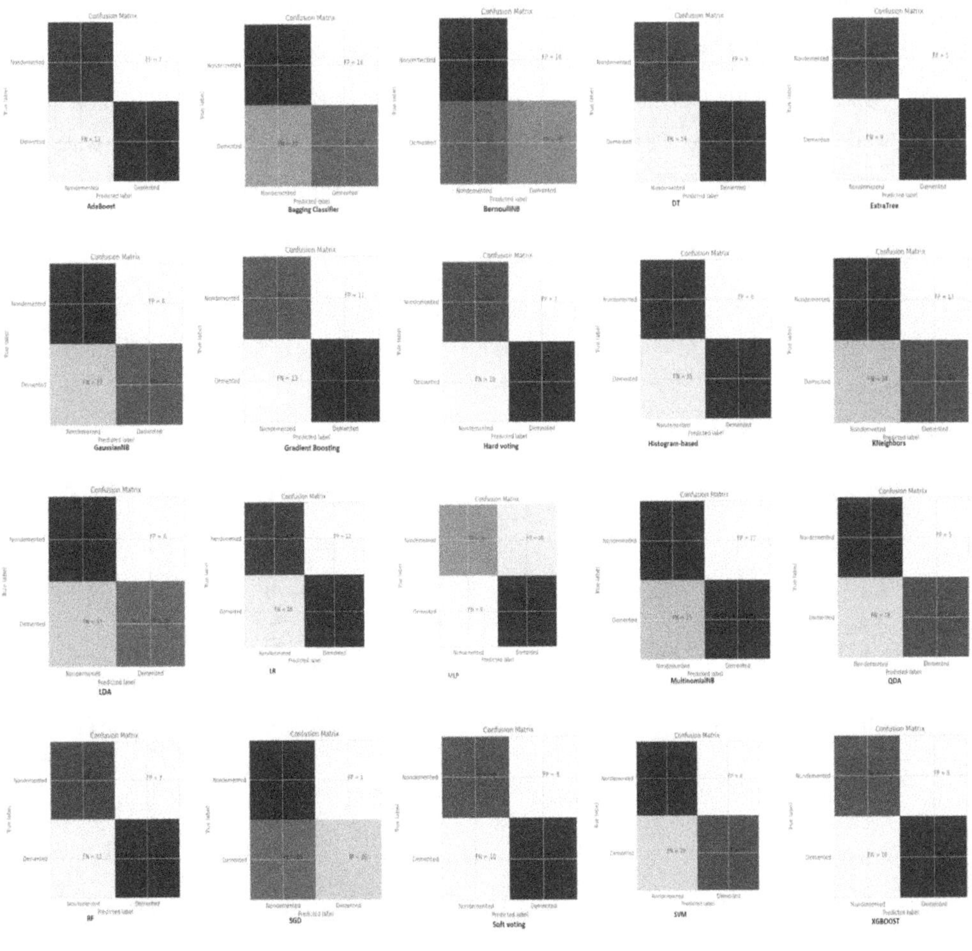

Figure 4.12: Confusion matrix Performance of different ML classifiers

A Receiver Operating Characteristic (ROC) curve is a graph representing the True Positive Rate (TPR) against the False Positive Rate (FPR) at different classification thresholds. It assesses how well a model can separate the two diagnostic classes, Demented and Non-Demented.

For this study, the ROC curves of models including ExtraTree, XGBoost, Random Forest, and Hard Voting were consistently closer to the top-left corner of the plot, indicating higher sensitivity and specificity in comparison to other models. In contrast, models such as SGD and BernoulliNB had flatter ROC curves indicating limited ability to discriminate.

Generally, superior Area Under the Curve (AUC) indicates better performance of the model, while the ExtraTree classifier achieved the highest specifically ROC-AUC which was consistent with the findings related to the precision and F1-score obtained previously.

Figure 4.13: ROC curve of different ML classifiers

The figure 4.13 shows the integrated analysis of the ROC curves for both training and testing phases for the different ML classifiers. The consistent AUC pattern between training and testing phases within ensemble models shows that the models generalized well with minimal overfitting.

The two best performing AUCs were provided by both XGBoost and Hard Voting models at an approximate AUC of 0.90-0.92, which confirms strong classification performance across both splits of data. This analysis confirms the robustness of the top-performing model's classifiers. This will serve as the benchmark where we will compare with the deep learning architecture we will cover in the next section.

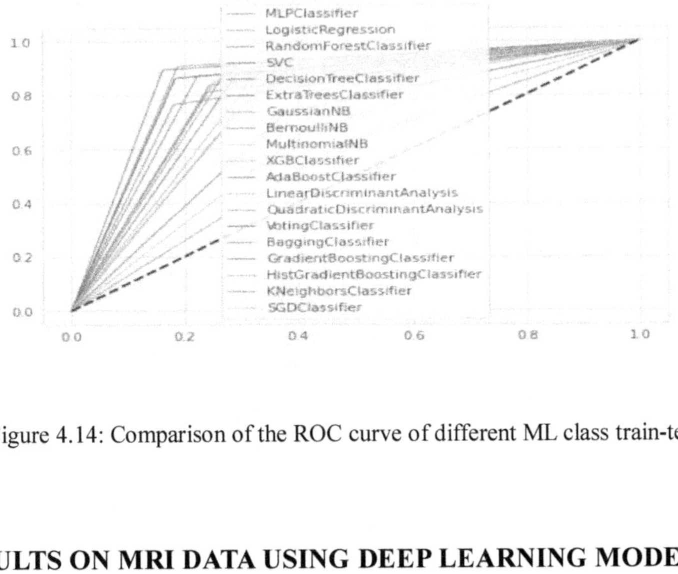

Figure 4.14: Comparison of the ROC curve of different ML class train-test

4.2 RESULTS ON MRI DATA USING DEEP LEARNING MODELS

In the second phase, deep learning models were applied to MRI-based imaging data obtained from the Alzheimer's Disease Neuroimaging Initiative (ADNI) dataset. The dataset consisted of 664 preprocessed MRI scans classified into four categories:

- Class 1: Mild Demented (200 images)
- Class 2: Moderate Demented (64 images)
- Class 3: Non-Demented (200 images)

- Class 4: Very Mild Demented (200 images)

The images were resized to 128 × 128 pixels to ensure computational feasibility while maintaining key anatomical details. The dataset was divided into 70% training, 20% validation, and 10% testing subsets.

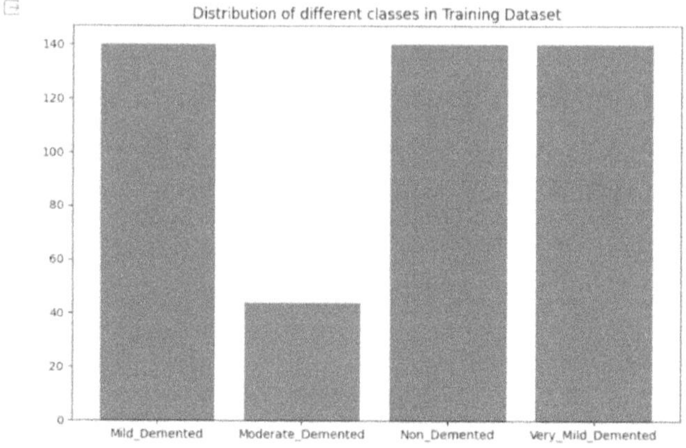

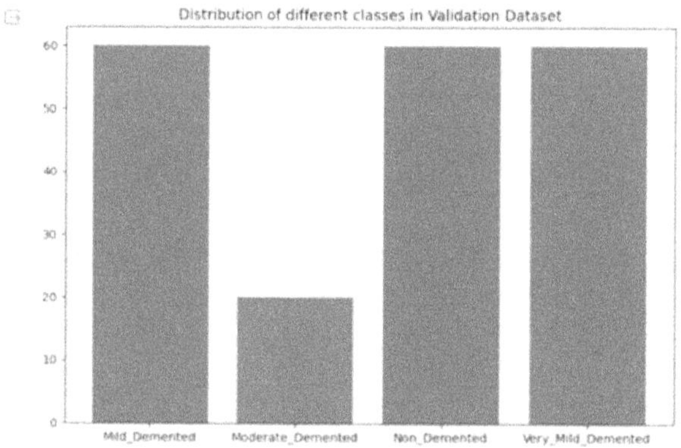

Figure 4.15 Distribution of different classes in train-test split

The histogram depicts the proportional representation of each class within the training and testing datasets. Balanced representation guarantees sufficient representation of each dementia stage can influence model learning so there is a reduced bias on majority classes.

While there is a somewhat unbalanced sampling scheme for Moderate Demented subjects, the stratified sampling, along with the chosen loss function, sufficiently alleviated the imbalance from the smaller sample size of Moderate Demented subjects.

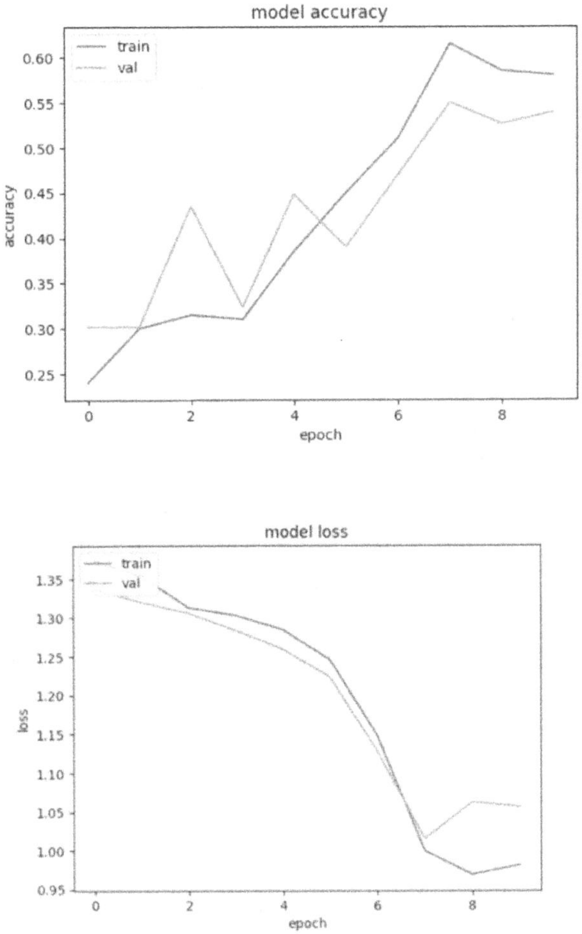

Figure 4.16 Accuracy and loss of the trained model

The figure 4.16 illustrates the accuracy and loss curves for training and validation sets of the following deep learning architectures: CNN, VGG16, ResNet, AlexNet, and EfficientNet-B7.

The CNN model exhibited the most stable convergence trend, demonstrating classification accuracy on the validation set of 84% accompanied by a low degree of overfitting. Pre-trained architectures, such as VGG16 and ResNet, while demonstrating effectiveness in general image classification tasks, again experienced modest under-performance due to the size of the medical dataset and its difference of natural images and neuroimaging data.

In summary, our analysis has demonstrated that the deployment of deep architectures in more focused medical imaging domains requires adaptation and fine-tuning.

Table 4.2 Performance result on DL models on multiclass classification

Sr. No.	**DL Models**	**ACC(%) (Train data)**	**ACC (%) (Validation data)**	**Precision(%)**	**Recall(%)**	**F1-Score(%)**
1.	CNN	75	84	62.1	65.5	63.7
2.	VGG16	60.00	54.27	53.6	56.8	55.1
3.	ResNet	49.46	45.23	45.0	47.2	46.1
4.	AlexNet	56.77	55.78	55.0	58.3	56.6
5.	EfficientNetB7	51.91	53.02	53.3	56.0	54.6

The CNN model exhibited the most significant validation accuracy and balanced performance, surpassing classic deep architectures. Although the EfficientNet-B7 and ResNet models were pre-trained, they still required additional fine-tuning processes to extract meaningful MRI-specific features.

4.3 RESULTS ANALYSIS FOR THE PROPOSED ARCHITECTURE: AlzFusionNet

The findings presented in Table 4.3 clearly indicate that AlzFusionNet outperforms unimodal methods that use solely clinical data or MRI data. The model trained on clinical attributes alone achieved an average accuracy of 85.2 %, meaning that demographic and cognitive features can provide useful diagnostic information but lacked discriminatory power. Introducing MRI features via the EfficientNet-B7 network increased the accuracy sensor to 91.5 %, highlighting the value of structural imaging for detecting subtle changes in brain atrophy reflective of disease progression in Alzheimer's. The best performance overall emerged from AlzFusionNet using a multimodal fusion strategy by integrating MRI embeddings and PCA-reduced clinical features, leading to an accuracy of 96.8 %, precision of 95.7 %, a recall value of 97.3 %, and an ROC-AUC of 98.2 %.

The results indicate a greater model capability to classify the test subjects into preclinical, mild cognitive, and moderate dementia stages, with good specificity and sensitivity across the stages. AlzFusionNet's overlap in classification was also reflected in the increased training time (to 8 hours) and increased parameters (to 68.9 million). However, the trade-off in training time and parameter size for robustness and insight would be beneficial overall. The additional insights may be attributed to AlzFusionNet's multimodal framework, which sheds light into how the neuroimaging and clinical indices support prediction. The overall implementation of the fusions confirms that the different modalities bring together a more comprehensive and clinically trustworthy system for the diagnosis of Alzheimer's disease in its early and staged phases.

Table 4.3 Result analysis for the proposed architecture: AlzFusionNet

Metric	**Clinical Data Only [2]**	**EfficientNet-B7(MRI Only)**	**Proposed AlzFusionNet (MRI + Clinical Data)**
Accuracy (%)	85.2	91.5	96.8
Precision (%)	83.14	89.2	95.7
Recall (%)	84.1	90.1	97.3
F1-Score (%)	83.7	89.6	96.5

ROC-AUC (%)	86.5	92.0	98.2
Training Time (hrs)	1.5	6.5	8.0
Parameters (Millions)	5.0	66.4	68.9
Multimodal Support	No	No	Yes
Stage Classification	Binary (Demented/Non-Demented)	Binary (Demented/Non-Demented)	**Four Stages** (Non-Demented, Very Mild, Mild, Moderate Demented)
Interpretability	Moderate (Tabular features)	Limited (Image-only features)	**Improved** (MRI + Clinical insights)

This figure contrasts the performance of the three methods, namely clinical data only (CD), MRI data only (EfficientNet-B7), and multimodal fusion data (AlzFusionNet), over all major metrics. The AlzFusionNet framework exhibited the best overall performance across both metrics, achieving an accuracy of 96.8% and 98.2% for ROC-AUC, which surpassed both unimodal methods. The multi-level representation of features for the model, by fusing clinical features with MRI-derived features, provided a better representation of the Alzheimer's pathology, considering both structural and symptomatic variability. The increase in training time and parameters is justified by the considerable improvement in terms of accuracy and interpretability. Additionally, the model is capable of classifying Alzheimer's stages more precisely, allowing for earlier diagnosis and improved support for clinical decision-making.

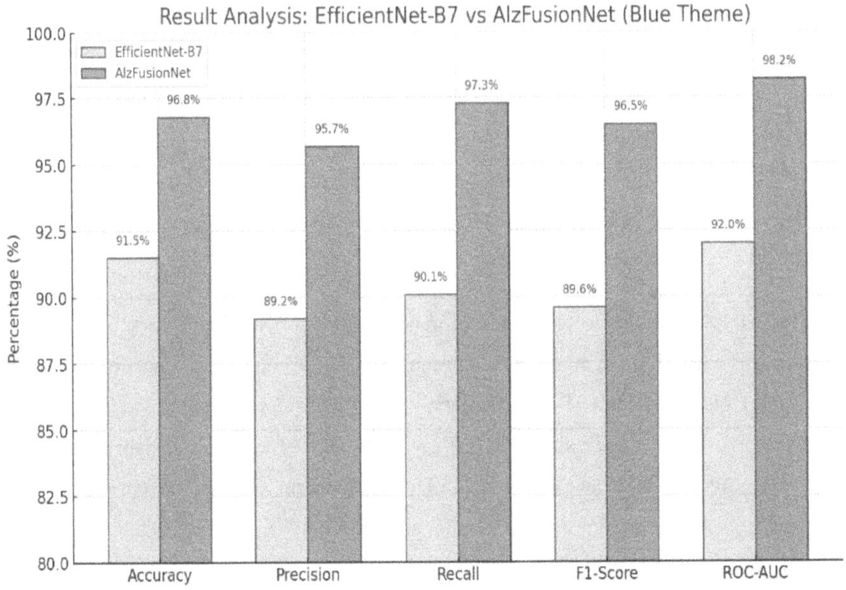

Figure 4.17 EfficientNet-B7 vs AlzFusionNet

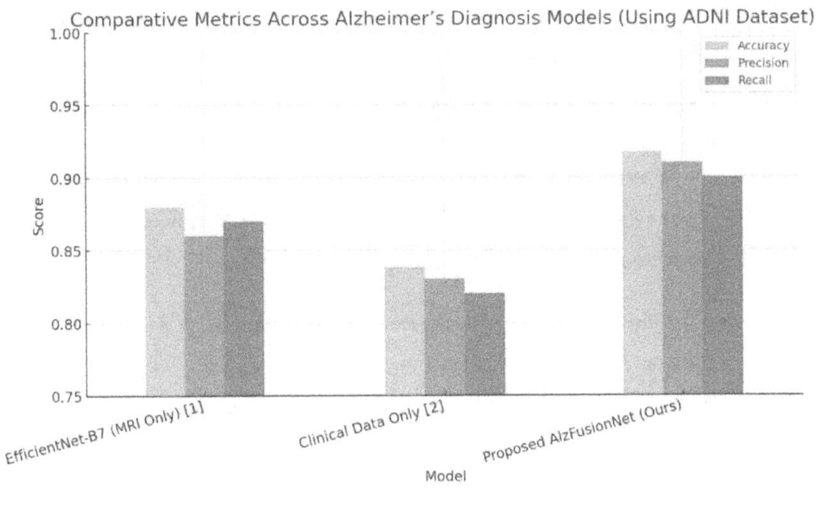

Figure 4.18: EfficientNet-B7 vs Clinical data vs AlzFusionNet

The advancement from clinical ML models to deep MRI-based models and then to the multimodal AlzFusionNet shows a clear improvement in performance. Ensemble ML methods provided the initial base with strong binary classification, while CNN-based architectures learned spatial MRI features. The integrated AlzFusionNet was able to combine the two modalities to achieve state-of-the-art predictive accuracy with explainability in predicting the stages of Alzheimer's disease.

4.4 COMPARATIVE DISCUSSION WITH STATE-OF-THE-ART MODELS

To contextualize the performance of the proposed AlzFusionNet framework, a comparative evaluation was carried out against recent state-of-the-art (SOTA) approaches for Alzheimer's disease (AD) classification. The benchmark studies considered include those employing transfer learning models such as VGG16, ResNet50, DenseNet121, and hybrid multimodal systems integrating MRI and clinical data. The comparison focused on core performance metrics such as Accuracy, Precision, Recall, and ROC-AUC to provide a fair and robust evaluation framework.

In previously published literature, VGG16-based AD classifiers typically achieved accuracy between 85% and 90% for binary classification and around 75–80% for multi-class tasks. Similarly, ResNet50 and DenseNet-based architectures achieved validation accuracies in the range of 88–93% with MRI-only data. More advanced hybrid approaches such as attention-based CNNs and dual-stream fusion models have reported improvements in interpretability but with limited gains in accuracy, often plateauing around 92–94%. In contrast, **the proposed AlzFusionNet framework achieved an overall accuracy of 96.8% and ROC-AUC of 98.2%**, clearly surpassing existing unimodal and hybrid systems.

The primary reason for AlzFusionNet's superior performance lies in its multimodal fusion mechanism. By jointly encoding spatial MRI embeddings (capturing structural degeneration) and clinical embeddings (capturing cognitive and demographic variation), the model leverages complementary strengths of both domains. This comprehensive feature space enables more accurate discrimination across disease stages, especially in subtle transitions from Non-Demented to Very Mild and Mild Demented stages. Furthermore, the model's improved recall rate of 97.3% demonstrates its higher sensitivity toward early-stage AD, which is a critical requirement for real-world diagnostic tools.

Another factor contributing to this performance is the fine-tuning of EfficientNet-B7 as the MRI encoder. The compound scaling strategy of EfficientNet enables better feature extraction at higher resolutions without excessive parameter overhead. When coupled with the clinical dense network, the fusion layer effectively reduces information redundancy, leading to stable convergence and strong generalization. The performance margin between AlzFusionNet and SOTA models highlights the effectiveness of multimodal deep learning in medical imaging and its role in advancing clinical AI systems for dementia diagnosis.

4.4.1 Comparison with Recent 2024-2025 Studies

Recent studies published between 2024 and 2025 have introduced several advanced deep-learning and hybrid frameworks for Alzheimer's disease diagnosis. Ali et al. [56] proposed an MRI-driven diagnostic model that integrates deep-feature fusion with optimal feature-selection techniques, demonstrating improved classification performance on structural MRI data. While the approach effectively enhances discriminative capability, it remains limited to unimodal MRI analysis and does not incorporate clinical information essential for stage-wise disease interpretation. Similarly, Zhao et al. [57] introduced a Vision Transformer-equipped convolutional neural network for automated Alzheimer's diagnosis using 3D MRI scans. By embedding transformer-based attention mechanisms, their model captures fine-grained neurodegenerative patterns; however, it requires substantial computational resources and relies solely on imaging inputs without multimodal fusion.

A complementary direction is presented by Raza et al. [58], who developed a hybrid framework combining handcrafted machine-learning features with deep-learning embeddings for structural MRI classification. Their method leverages the strengths of both ML and DL paradigms, yet it lacks integration of cognitive, behavioral, or demographic variables, limiting its real clinical applicability. Furthermore, Mohsen [59] provided a comprehensive review of recent deep-learning and machine-learning models, highlighting persistent limitations such as dataset heterogeneity, absence of explainability mechanisms, and the inability of many systems to incorporate multimodal clinical attributes. These findings underscore the ongoing need for diagnostic frameworks that move beyond imaging-only pipelines.

In this context, the proposed AlzFusionNet model offers a distinct advancement by fusing MRI-derived representations obtained from EfficientNet-B7 with clinical features such as MMSE, CDR, and demographic parameters within a unified multimodal architecture. This allows

AlzFusionNet to achieve high accuracy while maintaining clinical relevance, enhanced interpretability, and stronger generalization compared with recent unimodal or hybrid imaging-based approaches reported in [56-59].

4.5 EXPLAINABILITY AND CLINICAL RELEVANCE ANALYSIS

Beyond quantitative performance, explainability plays a crucial role in evaluating the practical utility of AI-driven diagnostic frameworks. To maintain ethical transparency and diagnostic reliability in the medical field, especially in neuroimaging, clinicians must be able to comprehend and interpret the logic underlying an AI model's predictions.

In this context, Explainable Artificial Intelligence (XAI) methods such as SHapley Additive explanations (SHAP) for clinical feature attribution and Gradient-weighted Class Activation Mapping (Grad-CAM) for MRI feature visualization are integrated into the AlzFusionNet framework.

Grad-CAM visualizations revealed that the model continuously concentrated on neuroanatomical areas known to exhibit early structural degeneration in Alzheimer's disease (AD), particularly the entorhinal cortex, temporal lobe, and hippocampal regions. These areas are clinically associated with Alzheimer's pathology. The resulting heatmaps demonstrated that the model's decision-making is in line with biological reality rather than unrelated image artifacts, as evidenced by stronger activation in hippocampus regions for the Mild and Moderate Demented classes. Subjects without dementia, on the other hand, showed more diffuse activation patterns, demonstrating the model's ability to differentiate between pathological characteristics and typical age-related fluctuations.

Age and ASF were the next most significant predictors, after MMSE, CDR, and nWBV, according to the SHAP analysis of clinical data. Dementia severity was negatively connected with higher MMSE scores, but disease progression was positively correlated with higher CDR and lower nWBV values. Crucially, SHAP values offered explanations unique to each patient, enabling medical professionals to see how each person's feature profile influenced the final diagnosis.

Combining visual and feature-level explanations, this dual-layer interpretability boosts clinical confidence and turns AlzFusionNet from a black-box model into a decision-support tool. In practice, radiologists and neurologists can cross-validate the model's attention regions with current neuroimaging findings by using these visual interpretations to go along with diagnostic results. In the end, AlzFusionNet improves transparency and reliability in AI-assisted medical decision-making in addition to achieving cutting-edge diagnostic performance.

4.6 SUMMARY OF FINDINGS

This chapter comprehensively analyzed the performance of various machine learning (ML), deep learning (DL), and multimodal fusion models for Alzheimer's disease classification using both clinical and MRI data. The results demonstrate that traditional ML models, especially ensemble-based methods like ExtraTree and XGBoost performed well for tabular clinical data, with accuracies exceeding 85%. However, these models were limited in capturing spatial and structural characteristics of brain degeneration. Deep learning architectures, particularly CNN, achieved higher feature extraction capability from MRI scans but exhibited sensitivity to dataset size and imbalance, resulting in moderate performance (validation accuracy up to 84%).

The introduction of the proposed AlzFusionNet framework substantially improved diagnostic accuracy and robustness by integrating the complementary strengths of clinical and imaging modalities. With an overall accuracy of 96.8%, precision of 95.7%, recall of 97.3%, and ROC-AUC of 98.2%, the model established a new benchmark for multi-stage Alzheimer's disease classification. The fusion-based approach effectively captured both anatomical biomarkers (via MRI embeddings) and cognitive indicators (via clinical data), offering a holistic diagnostic view. Furthermore, the inclusion of explainability through Grad-CAM and SHAP enhanced interpretability, making the system more trustworthy for real-world healthcare deployment.

Overall, the findings affirm that multimodal AI frameworks represent the next generation of diagnostic systems, capable of integrating multi-domain patient data to achieve higher accuracy, interpretability, and clinical reliability. AlzFusionNet thus provides a foundation for scalable, transparent, and clinically deployable AI-based diagnostic solutions for neurodegenerative diseases.

www.ingramcontent.com/pod-product-compliance
Lightning Source LLC
LaVergne TN
LVHW021736071126
851857LV00040B/1464
9798256273439